An Engineer Officer Under Wellington in the Peninsular

The Diary and Correspondence
of Lieut. Rice Jones, R. E.
During 1808-9-10-11-12.

Edited by Cdr. The Hon. Henry N.
Shore, R. N.

As published in the Royal Engineers Journal
Volumes XVI and XVII,
1912-1913

2023
Waterville, Maine
pagesofpages.com

The illustration reproduced on the cover, "A field officer of the Royal Engineers with a private Sapper. 1812." is by Charles Hamilton Smith, and from *Costumes of the Army of the British Empire, according to the last regulations 1812.* London: Colnaghi and Company, 1812-1815.

Publisher's Note

Rice Jones, the writer of the diary and of most of the letters contained in this volume was a young officer in the Royal Engineers when he was sent to Portugal in 1809. He remained until 1812, ending his peninsular experiences at Ciudad Rodrigo where he successfully lead the 52nd and 43rd regiments into one of the lesser breaches. His other main experiences were the Battle of Bussaco, the building of the Lines of Torres Vedras, and the abortive siege of Badajoz in early 1811. Writing of Rice Jones's role at Ciudad Rodrigo, the editor remarks "Of this exploit, our diarist supplies the briefest and most modest narrative that was probably ever penned by a son to his father."

These papers were first published in volumes XVI and XVII of the Royal Engineers Journal, 1912 and 1913. The editor, H. V. [sic] Shore, was Henry Noel Shore, Fifth Baron Teignmouth[1], author of several books ("Smuggling Days and Smuggling Ways", etc.), and by 1912 a retired Commander of the Royal Navy. The first issue of the Royal Engineers Journal had him as Captain H. V. Shore, late of the Royal Navy, which was corrected in later issues. The original accreditation is shown at the beginning of chapter one.

The contents from the nine issues are here labeled as separate chapters. Shore provides general background to the author's experiences, comparisons with other accounts of events, and summaries of diary entries that were, in his view, not of enough professional or historical interest to include in their entirety.

Charles Oman makes reference of these documents in an appendix to Volume 5 of his *History of the Peninsular War*, "Notes on some points of controversy regarding the storm of Ciudad Rodrigo" (page 589-590).

---

[1] Henry N. Shore's father, Charles John Shore, Second Baron Teignmouth, published an autobiography, *Reminiscences of Many Years* (1878), that contains an interesting chapter on Waterloo. Shore was invited to visit Lord Hill's headquarters in Grammont and arrived with one of Hill's brothers a few days before the battle. He describes the social scene just prior to the battle, the confusion of troop movements, and then the rumors and chaos during and immediately after the battle. He was in Paris in time to see Wellington's entry into the city.

Shore also provides a sketch of Rice Jones's later career. From Hart's New Annual Army List and Militia List we can add the dates of each of his ranks. He was appointed Second Lieutenant Feb 1, 1806; First Lieutenant Jul 1, 1806; Captain May 1, 1811; Lieutenant Colonel Jun 8, 1830; and Colonel Nov 9, 1846. As of his last appearance in Hart's (1854) he had 46 years of service at full pay, and 2 years 8 months on half pay. Promotion in the Royal Engineers was by seniority; commissions were not purchased (and therefore could not be sold to fund a retirement). Jones had a long career, but his not-quite 49 years in 1855 pales when compared to the three Royal Engineer Colonels who were then senior, each with 61 years of service, and a date of first appointment in 1793.

Other contemporary accounts written by Jones's engineer colleagues include the following.

Charles Boothby. *A Prisoner of France* (1898). *Under England's Flag* (1900).

John Fox Burgoyne. *Life and Correspondence* (1873).

John T. Jones. *Journals of Sieges Carried on by the Army under the Duke of Wellington in Spain During the Years 1811-1814* (1827). *Memoranda Relative to the Lines Thrown Up to Cover Lisbon in 1810* (1829).

George T. Landmann. *Adventures and Recollections of Colonel Landmann, Late of the Corps of Royal Engineers* (1852). *Recollections of My Military Life* (1854).

Contents

AN ENGINEER OFFICER UNDER WELLINGTON IN THE PENINSULA.

THE DIARY AND CORRESPONDENCE OF LIEUT. RICE JONES, R.E., DURING 1808-9-10-11-12.

WITH LETTERS FROM DISTINGUISHED OFFICERS AT THE SEAT OF WAR IN PORTUGAL, SPAIN, FRANCE, BELGIUM, AND AMERICA AND AFTERWARDS.

(Edited by CAPT. THE HON. H. V. SHORE, LATE R.N.).

INTRODUCTORY.

IT is meet and right that we should be reminded, from time to time, of the protracted and exhausting struggle that was maintained by our forebears a hundred years ago, on behalf of the Peninsular nations and in the cause of European freedom, against the Napoleonic usurpation. And no form of reminder proves more acceptable than the personal experiences of men who bore a part in that momentous struggle. For these narratives—no matter how defective they may be from a literary point of view—convey a much more vivid picture of war ; the hardships, sufferings, and strenuous labours of those engaged, to say nothing of the miseries, most patiently endured, by the innocent and unoffending inhabitants of territories involved, than can be derived from the nicely balanced sentences, the polished periods, and the fine language of the professional historian, be he never so learned.

The author of the Diary and Letters, which form the groundwork of the present series, first embarked for foreign service with General Whitelocke's ill-starred expedition to Buenos Ayres. But the operations having been brought to a close before his arrival, there was nothing to be done but to return home, where, shortly afterwards, he was a witness of the landing at Falmouth, of some of the débris of Sir John Moore's unfortunate army. He was now ordered to Portugal, and joined the army which was assembling at Coimbra, just before the arrival of Sir Arthur Wellesley to take command, for the second time, of the British forces in the Peninsula. During the Oporto Campaign which ensued, he was on the staff of Colonel Fletcher, the Commanding Royal Engineer, which brought him into close attendance on Sir A. Wellesley during the whole of the operations. During the Talavera Campaign, he enjoyed the same privileged position ; and as soon as Sir Arthur had decided, in consultation with his Chief Engineer on the construction of that tremendous defensive

position across the Lisbon peninsula, he found employment during
the winter of 1809-10 in superintending the works destined to form
the western end of the afterwards famous "LINES OF TORRES
VEDRAS." During the summer of 1810, the work on the Lines being
well advanced, our diarist accompanied his commanding officer to
rejoin the army in the field, *vis-à-vis* of Massena's invading host, and
was present, in close attendance on Lord Wellington, at the Battle of
Busaco, and during the operations connected with the retreat of the
allied forces within the Lines. Following in the wake of Massena's
retreat, in the spring of 1811, he took part in the first abortive Siege
of Badajoz ; accompanied his commanding officer to the field of
Albuera, which was reached just at the close of the action ; took part
in the second Siege of Badajoz ; and after it was raised, joined the
Light Division, and, during the remaining months of 1811, was on the
staff of General Robert Craufurd whom he accompanied on his many
hazardous reconnaissances around Ciudad Rodrigo. By the directions
of that officer he accompanied the storming party of the Light
Division, at the assault of Ciudad Rodrigo, in January, 1812, on which
glorious occasion (to quote his own words) " he had the good fortune
to lead the 52nd and 43rd Regiments to a small breach, to the left of
the large one." Of this exploit, our diarist supplies the briefest and
most modest narrative that was probably ever penned by a son to his
father. This thrilling episode formed a fitting conclusion to his service
with the Peninsular Army. He returned home immediately afterwards, to take up the post of Adjutant at Woolwich, where, later, he
performed the duties of Brigade Major ; and after holding various
responsible posts in Nova Scotia, Dover and Malta, he died at the
age of 64, when Commanding Royal Engineer at Gibraltar, in 1854.

Not the least of the interest attaching to these records of war
service is the fresh light they throw on many disputed points, and
especially on the personal qualities and disposition of the celebrated
leader of the Light Division, General Robert Craufurd, with whom
our diarist would seem to have been on terms of the closest intimacy
during several months, at a critical stage of the war, and whose loss at
the storm of Rodrigo he deplores in almost affectionate words. It
will certainly be news to most people to learn that that fiery warrior,
and stern disciplinarian " kept one of the best tables in the army."

During his service in the Peninsula, the diarist contracted many
warm and lasting friendships ; not alone with his contemporaries, but
with officers of standing under whom he served, and who continued
to correspond with him up to the time of his death. The friendly
and intimate letters written by his late chief, Sir Richard Fletcher,
Sir J. T. Jones, and Sir John Burgoyne, from the seat of war, to
the young Adjutant of Engineers at Woolwich (he was only 23 when
he took up the post) are by no means the least illuminative, or
interesting portion of the volume. The last of the series is from

that distinguished Engineer, Sir John Burgoyne, on the eve of the Crimean War, in which struggle he was destined to play a prominent part.

Rice Jones, the author of the Diary, was born May 29th, 1788. Electing to follow his father's profession he was placed, in due course, at the Royal Military Academy, Woolwich, whence he joined the Royal Engineers, January, 1807.

That the educational requirements of a youth, on entering the Academy, in those distant times, were not of a high order may be gathered from some letters written by a young Engineer officer, while serving under the Duke of York, in the Netherlands, to a near relative, with reference to the entry of his younger brother at the Academy :—

CAMP NEAR EN LE FONTAINE,
October 22nd, 1793.

I had a letter from my mother by last post, in which she tells me that the Duke had written to her, that he would make Kenneth a Cadet in February. As a great deal depends on getting off well at first, I shall write you a few instructions about what he should learn, which you will be so good as to communicate to his master. He must pay particular attention to his Arithmetick. I suppose he is already master of the Rule of Three. He must next learn Vulgar and Decimal Fractions with the Extraction of the Square and Cube Roots. This is what he is required to know to qualify him for admission into the Academy. So that he must be master of these before he goes on farther. After that he may learn Arithmetical and Geometrical Progression with Single and Double Position. Get for him *Hutton's Arithmetick*, as it is the book taught in the Academy, and if he learns another the Masters will probably make him begin over again. As he goes on he must write the Rules and Examples in a book, and take care to keep it clean and neatly written : this he must show when examined for admission to the Academy. I would not have him discontinue his Latin, (though the principal attention should be paid to his Writing and Arithmetick), it will facilitate his learning other languages ; and the learning passages by heart will strengthen his memory, and will be of great service to him in getting thro' the Academy. As to French, he had better not begin it till he gets to the Academy ; for what he could learn now would not be of much service to him, considering the change of Masters and Grammers, except he has much spare time on his hands. If he pays attention to his studies, and is not idle when he first goes to the Academy, he may have an opportunity of getting before many of those who are admitted at the same time, which will make the difference of years when he gets to the top of the Academy.

A month later he returns to the subject :—

GHENT, November 29th, 1793.

I wrote to you some time ago, I hope you got the letter, as it mentioned something about Kenneth's studies—understanding from my mother that he is going to Woolwich in February. I would have him now transcribe from *Hutton's Arithmetick* (beginning with Vulgar Fractions) what I mentioned in my last letter, in a Folio Blank Book. If he writes this well and keeps his book clean, it may be allowed to pass when he goes to the Academy. This will advance him four or five months, besides is a great thing, as they now remain so short a time at the Academy. This is a good time to go there ; a number of commissions are now vacant, and more likely to be won, as an augmentation of Artillery is going to take place ; indeed the Duke has been obliged to give away nine to people who have not been to the Academy. . . .

Writing again, under date, October 8th, 1795, he says :—"I have seen Kenneth. He has been very idle and near been dismissed ; but I believe is now doing better, and I hope will get away before next summer. . . ."

(NOTE.—Before three years had passed, both these fine young men—one in the Royal Engineers, the other in the Artillery, had succumbed to yellow fever in the West Indies).

The Diaries, which form the groundwork of the following pages, are in a clear, small, copperplate handwriting, often so minute as almost to require the aid of a magnifying glass for their elucidation, but all penned with equal care, whether in barracks at home, or on active service in the field. Whence may be inferred a love of method, neatness, regularity, and perseverance. The first entry bears the date, January 19th, 1807 ; the last, December 31st, 1816 ; and the whole are contained in three small note-books, bound in red.

The first three months of service were passed uneventfully at headquarters, at Chatham, whence frequent excursions on horseback were made to Hythe, where a brother resided. Once, he made a trip, " with Capt. Cunningham, Royal Engineers, to see the towers and works on the coast." The *raison d'être* of these works, which had been carried out by the eminent engineer, George Rennie, and would naturally be of considerable professional interest to a young officer of the scientific Corps, is thus explained by Smiles, in *The Lives of the Engineers*. During the invasion scare of 1803, Mr. Rennie, as the first engineer of the day, was invited by Government to draw up a scheme for flooding the valley of the Lea :—the eastern side of the metropolis being considered the most accessible to an invading force landing at the mouth of the Thames. The works, however, were only partially executed ; Napoleon having changed his plans in the interim. But in 1806, when he was, once more, concentrating on the heights of Boulogne, Mr. Rennie was instructed to excavate a military canal from Hythe to Rye, encircling Romney Marsh, as that rich tract of pasture land is still inaptly styled. It was in connection with this work that Mr. Rennie came to loggerheads with the Ordnance Department. On his demanding seven guineas a day for his services it was pointed out to him that this was equivalent to the pay of a Field Marshal. Mr. Rennie replied that he considered himself a Field Marshal in his own profession, and, as he refused to make any abatement, the claim was paid in full.

The Martello Towers—as they are called, which still decorate our coast, from Folkestone westwards, were erected at the same period, costing, it is said, £40,000 a piece. As their origin is not generally known it may be well to state that the idea was borrowed from a tower in Martello Bay, Corsica, which, with a single gun, on February 8th, 1794, beat off a combined attack by the 74-gun ship *Fortitude*, and the 32-gun frigate *Juno*. These two ships, notwithstanding their enormous superiority in guns, had to draw off after two hours and a-half steady firing; the former with the loss of 6 killed and 56 wounded, and having been set on fire. Two years afterwards, Capt. Jervis (better known as Earl St. Vincent), in a report to Admiral Young, dated H.M.S. *Victory*, Martello Bay, October 29th, 1796, wrote :—" I have the satisfaction to acquaint you that Martello Tower is reduced to a heap of fragments. Besides the advantage His Majesty's ships, will derive from the downfall of this powerful though simple fortification, I feel as if offering a sacrifice to the names of the gallant fellows who fell in the spirited attack you made upon it in the *Fortitude*." And he went on to state—what is of peculiar significance in view of his well-known antagonism to elaborate coast fortification and the prominent part he afterwards took in opposing the costly schemes of the Royal Engineers :—" Capt. Packenham is preparing a model and section of it (the Tower) to be presented to Marquis Cornwallis ; and I hope to see such works erected on all the ports the Duke of Richmond proposed to fortify with citadels requiring two thousand men to defend them, and on every part of the coast likely for the enemy to make a descent on. These works will require no garrison in time of peace, and very few men, as you have experienced, when besieged and attacked by sea and by land."

In the *Century Dictionary* we find the following definite statement on the subject :—" The efficiency of this work (in Corsica) induced the British authorities to build a large number of Martello Towers on their coasts, especially opposite France, in anticipation of Napoleon's threatened invasion."

The only useful purpose ever served by these towers was affording shelter for parties of seamen employed in the coast blockade, during the years 1816–31, and subsequently for the coastguardmen.

Within two months of joining the Corps, Rice Jones was ordered to accompany General Whitelocke's unfortunate expedition to S. America, and sailed from Spithead on March 9th, 1807. The transports put in to the Canaries, where they lay for six days ; but " Brigadier-General Acland ordered no officers or soldiers to go ashore." Sailing thence on April 13th, they had a long and dreary passage of more than three months before reaching their destination. "April 30th, made the coast of Brazil in 6–30 S. Lat. By the different reckonings we were 300 miles to the eastward; should have allowed for a current to the westward of about 1 mile per hour, mean rate.

May 1st, put on an allowance of water. May 23rd. Our fresh stock being finished were obliged to live upon salt provisions for the remainder of the voyage."

Not till July 23rd did they anchor in Maldonado Harbour; having crossed the line no less than three times, *en route*. On arrival " heard of our disaster in S. America."

From the fact of there being only one entry from the day of arrival at Monte Video till the force re-embarked, on September 9th; viz. :—" Took a section of the hill of Monte Video "; one gathers that the author saw no fighting. On the date above-named he " embarked about 11 a.m., with Capt. Dickson's Company of Royal Artillery, and went out of harbour." Little did Jones —or any other of Capt. Dickson's shipmates—foresee the brilliant career in store for that young Gunner, who, in six years time, was to command the whole of the Artillery of the Peninsular Army, under Lord Wellington.

The voyage home took three months; the transports anchoring in Cork Harbour December 17th. Here he heard, for the first time, of the death of his brother James, whom he last saw at Hythe, on April 1st.

The year 1808 was spent in England, chiefly on the east coast, in concerting measures of defence against invasion.

"April 16th. Taking sections of Hollesley Bay and marshes.

May 14th. Placed pickets in Hollesley Bay.

„ 23rd. Marched with Guards to Hollesley Bay and marked out the spots for them to encamp.

Sept. 2nd. Lieut. Loyalty Peake ordered to Landguard Fort.

„ 24th. I have been constantly going round the coast of Essex, sleeping either at St. Osyth, Gt. Clacton, or Thorpe."

Early in December he received orders to be ready to embark at the shortest notice; and, on reaching London learnt that he was to proceed to Portugal.

1809. While detained at Portsmouth, waiting for the sailing of the transports, the author, ever eager to improve his mind, " went with other officers to the Dockyard to see the machinery for making blocks." The beautiful piece of mechanism here alluded to, the invention of Mr. Brunel, had only recently been installed, through the influence of Lord St. Vincent. When the invention was first brought to the notice of the Navy Board, one of the members exclaimed "What! turn a thing oval!—no, that I never can nor will believe;

turn a thing round if you like ; but as to turning a thing oval, it is only wasting our time, and so there's an end of it."

The transports were nearly a week getting to Falmouth, where, on anchoring, those on board " heard the disastrous accounts from Spain, and saw several wounded men landing," the remnants of Sir John Moore's gallant force. Three days afterwards came news " that the *Primrose*, sloop of war (one of the escorting squadron), had run upon the Manacles Rocks on Sunday morning, when we made land, and that every soul on board perished except a little boy." The body of her unfortunate captain was recovered, and buried with military honours at Falmouth.

During the detention here of the transports, from January 24th to February 22nd, Rice Jones whiled away the time in taking long walks with brother officers; his most frequent companions being Capts. Chapman and Goldfinch, of the Royal Engineers ; the former, one gathers, was an artist, from the fact of his being left behind, on one occasion, at Flushing, to take a sketch. Opportunity was taken by the people around of the presence of so many young officers, to arrange various social functions, including many balls. Thus ;—" February 7th, Chapman and Goldfinch walked to the Ball at Penryn. I was prevented going by not having a good Regimental Coat here." Part of the baggage had got into a wrong transport at Portsmouth, and was not recovered until some months later. Again February 9th. "Chapman went to a Ball at Truro."—"February 16th. Walked to Penryn with the ladies who were at the ball last night." Again, " February 21st. Went to Ball at Penryn, and then walked to Falmouth,"—possibly in borrowed plumes ! By way of variety Jones and Goldfinch set off on a riding tour to the Land's End, returning by St. Ives, Camborne, and Redruth.

Sailing orders having at length arrived, the transports set sail for the Peninsula on February 24th ; arriving at Lisbon on March 4th, where young Jones was introduced by his commanding officer to the Commander-in-Chief, Sir J. Craddock. Two days later, he took up his billet at No. 12, Rua Largo de St. Roque. He was now appointed Adjutant to the Corps, in Portugal ; bought a horse, which his landlord had procured for him, for 210 dollars ; recovered his missing baggage ; saw the Guards reviewed in the Rocio ; and having received instructions from Capt. Chapman* to proceed along the right bank of the Tagus as far as Abrantes, and examine the ground about Thomar and Leyria, in company with Lieut. Stanway, he left Lisbon on March 21st, reaching Villa Franca the same evening— " where we were billetted on a tradesman and used very civilly." It is described as " a very neat little town in a valley, on the banks of the Tagus ; the ground in the neighbourhood beautifully varied with

* See Note 2, end of chapter.

vineyards, and orange and olive groves." Later on, this beautiful spot was ruthlessly destroyed by Massena's troops. Next evening they reached Santarem where they were billetted upon a fidalgo, "who was governor of some town, but who did not treat us very well." Next night was passed at Golegao, "in a small house, but used very well." But "their cookery most disgusting." And so on, through "a beautiful country—raining the best part of the day," to Abrantes, where they were quartered upon a priest, "who used us very kindly." Next night was spent at Punhete, owing to some Portuguese soldiers, holding a post on the opposite bank of the river Zezere, refusing to allow a boat to come over for the English officers. "We were billetted in a good house belonging to an old widow lady." The historic town of Thomar—their goal, was reached next day ; here they "were quartered upon a Tradesman who entertained us sump-tuously." An official call was paid on the Portuguese Governor, General Miranda, who "was very polite and ordered two Engineers to accompany us round the works and the old castle, etc." Thence on to Leyria, "the weather as usual rainy. Billetted upon an old lady who behaved very kindly to us." Of course, they inspected the castle of historic fame, and next day purposed visiting the celebrated monastery of Alcobaca ; "but mistaking the road, proceeded to Alcoente, where we arrived very wet and late, and were not able to procure anything to eat but bread and butter, and wine to drink." They returned to their quarters at Lisbon next day, "arriving there late and extremely wet."

Two days later, "Lt.-Col. Fletcher, Capt. Burgoyne, and Lts. Hamilton, Boothby, and Mulcaster landed here, and dined with us." The names of the first two officers will be familiar enough to stu-dents of the Peninsula Campaigns. Capt. Charles Boothby, a young Engineer officer of high promise, had the misfortune to lose his leg and his liberty at the Battle of Talavera, six months after landing, and remained a prisoner-of-war, in France, till July, 1810. His career as a soldier having been thus cut short, Boothby took Holy Orders, and was presented to the Crown living of Sutterton, in Lincolnshire, where he died in 1846. The story of his brief military career has been told by himself, in a book entitled *A Prisoner of France* (Adam and Charles Black, 1898).

TO HIS FATHER.

Addressed to :—
    Capt. R. Jones,
        Royal Denbigh Militia,
            Chatham.

Lisbon, *March* 5, 1809.

My Dear Father,

Yesterday morning we anchored safe off this place after a very pleasant voyage (if it is possible to call a voyage pleasant) we had good weather and fair wind most of the way, and it is reported that we had a narrow and fortunate escape from the French fleet, which they say here is now at sea; for all this I am very thankful and trust you are all well in England and Wales.

We sailed on the 22nd ult. and upon our getting out of the harbour of Falmouth we were taken under Convoy of the *Lavinia* Frigate, Capt. Lord Wm. Stuart, who was laying to for us, with a fleet of 19 sail from Plymouth consisting of merchantships, and transports with Artillery on board. As soon as we anchored Capt. Chapman and myself went ashore and waited upon the Commander-in-Chief, Sir John Craddock. Capt. Chapman has told me that if I like it, it was his wish that I should remain here with him; he is extremely kind and attentive to me, and I believe he intends taking me with him in whatever house he may be billetted. Our officers are billetted upon the inhabitants of this city, and have excellent rooms and accommodations; we get our quarters to-morrow. The British troops are all in this city and environs; they have lately been in constant readiness to embark; but no one seems to know where the French are, or whether this place is to be defended or not; since the arrival of General Beresford and ourselves, they seem to be rather more determined to defend it.

I fear we shall have some difficulty in mounting ourselves here, horses being not only dear but scarce; I am fearful I shall be obliged to draw upon you or Mr. R. Jones once more, as soon as I can find a decent beast, but make no doubt if we remain here I shall soon be able to remit it to you again. We are each allowed forage for three horses and a mule, and are to embark one horse each in case of this place being evacuated.

This is the most beautifully situated place I ever saw; the River Tagus is very fine all the way up. We have just walked to an immense Aqueduct near here, and have been regaling ourselves in a Vineyard and Orange Grove; the Vines are not yet in bud, but the oranges are excellent. The weather is as warm as the summer in England, and everything is in Blossom or bearing fruit. In my next I will give you a longer account, and will now conclude this by desiring my best love to my dear Mother and John, Mary, Anna, Eliza, Ebenezer, and Margaret.

Your loving son,
RICE JONES.

We have seen nothing of our baggage yet and begin to want it very much. Direct to me, " With the British Army in Portugal, Lisbon."—R.J.

LETTERS TO HIS FATHER.

LISBON, *March* 17, 1809.

MY DEAR FATHER,

On the 5th inst. I acquainted you with my safe arrival at this place, and have now the pleasure to inform you that I still continue in very good health. I am billetted in the Rua de San Roque, one of the pleasantest parts of the city; the house belongs to a Portuguese merchant named Don Bernade Silde; he is very civil to me; I have two rooms besides my bedroom and my servant's; I am the only officer that has ever been quartered upon him and he wanted to feed me at first, but I would not let him.° I find the little knowledge I have of Spanish of the greatest use to me, as it enables me (with the addition of what Portuguese I learn) to make myself understood in general.

This is a most delightful country at this time of the year; it is warm but not uncomfortably, and every thing is green, in blossom or bearing fruit.

The British troops have returned from Cadiz in consequence of the refusal at that place to admit them; they have disembarked at this place and environs; of course the detachment of our Corps destined for Cadiz has rejoined us.

You will I daresay be surprised to hear that I am once more doing the duty of Adjutant; in consequence of the great strength of our Corps here, and our having eight R.M. artificers, Capt. Chapman has appointed me to act as Adjutant to the Corps in Portugal, and has written to General Morse acquainting him with it and begging his approbation of the appointment. I am not very sanguine in my expectations of receiving the allowance for it; but I am glad of the situation inasmuch as my being chosen is flattering to myself, and also, it will keep me about Head Quarters with the Commanding Royal Engineer. There are 10 Engineers in this place at present, ... Capt. Chapman is ordered by Sir John Craddock to proceed into the interior to the neighbourhood of Thomar, Santarem, Abrantes, etc., to examine and report upon the ground there, as a position for an army intended to cover the approaches to Lisbon; he will set off to-day or to-morrow and I expect I shall accompany him with a detachment of our officers here; how long we shall be gone it is impossible to say; it is not improbable the army may soon follow us; at present they occupy a position at Lumiare, about 6 miles from here; it is a very good one, but is too near Lisbon to cover it effectually.

I have not yet been able to get a horse; it is however absolutely necessary before I can move from Lisbon; they are extremely dear and scarce. Capt. Chapman gave 50 guineas for one yesterday; it is hardly possible to get them for money; the French took most, and our army some; with the remainder every one is joining the Portuguese Army, for here every one is in arms. Capt. Chapman has represented this, as well as our want of allowance for servants, in the strongest manner to the Board; I wish it may have a good effect.

Please to give my best love to my dear Mother and my dear brothers and sisters. I am in hopes of soon hearing of your continued good health. Direct to me, " With the British Army in Portugal, Lisbon."

Your very loving son,
RICE JONES.

LISBON, April 5, 1809.

MY DEAR FATHER,

Since my last letter I have been reconnoitring the interior of this country.† I went from hence to Santarem, Abrantes, Thomar, Leyria,

---

° See Note 1, end of chapter.
† See Note 2.

etc., making a circuit of about 270 miles, and am now busy making out a Report upon the ground I passed; Lt. Stanway, a very young officer of ours, accompanied me; Capt. Chapman being obliged to remain in this place where we are commencing batteries on both sides of the Tagus; the Portuguese Engineers will I believe have the execution of those nearest Lisbon. It unfortunately rained every day I was absent from this place; but I am extremely glad I went, as in the event of our being obliged to evacuate this country, I may not have another opportunity of seeing it. We were billetted on the natives of every place we went to, and were in general very kindly treated, being the only English officers they had seen for some time; they were very anxious for the arrival of our troops, and received us with huzzas, etc., expecting that we were advanced and that the others were to follow us. It unluckily happened to be *Lent* all the time, consequently no one had anything to eat but fish; our food was regularly a fowl stewed in rice, and very oily. I could not bring my taste to like their dishes, but was unable to procure anything else: to complete our dislike we were always entertained soon after our arrival at any house, with the cries of the dying cock. I waited upon the Portuguese General Miranda at Thomar, who received me very kindly, showed me all the reports of his Quar.-Masr.-Genl. had upon the Position in that neighbourhood, and sent a Capt. and Subn. of Engineers to show me the batteries they were constructing. Every one in the country was armed, principally with Pikes; but after the termination of the boasted defence of Oporto, I am very dubious of their fighting. From our uniform being like the French we were sometimes mistaken for officers of that nation. A Portuguese outpost that had charge of a ferry boat across the river Zezere refused to come over for us, for all we could say or do, and we were obliged to go a great deal out of our way, to a bridge of boats. At every village we were desired by a guard of the natives armed with Pikes to show our Passports, but I seldom indulged them with a sight of it, and they never objected to our proceeding.

On my return I had the pleasure of finding a letter from you, and was happy to hear you are all well. I continue very well and have experienced no inconvenience, thank God, from the repeated wettings I had on my tour.

On Sunday Lt.-Col. Fletcher, Capt. Burgoyne and Lts. Hamilton, Boothby and Mulcaster arrived here from England, which is a very unfortunate circumstance, both to Capt. Chapman and myself, as he loses his Command and pay for it, and I lose the Adjutancy, Lt. Mulcaster having been appointed Adjt. and Qur. Mr. before he left England. I am certainly extremely unlucky; I shall lose by these officers' arrival three shillings a day.

Our baggage is at length arrived here; it was brought from Falmouth by a Merchant Schooner; I shall take care to profit by the lesson I have had and not part with my baggage so easily again.

Previous to my late journey I was of course obliged to purchase a horse, but he cost about double his real worth, owing to the great scarcity of horses; he is very strong, 7 years old and sound, but I cannot say much in favour of his beauty : he carried me remarkably well all the way. I gave 210 dollars (at 4s. 6d.) for him. The Ordnance Commissary has advanced me the money I wanted, so that I have not been under the necessity, I feared I should have been, to trouble you again. If we remain in this country I shall be able to clear my account soon, if not, I can but trouble you at the last.

All the troops are out of this city except the 87th, part of the Artillery and ourselves. The Head Qrs. is at Lumiar 6 miles off; but Sir J. Craddock has generally resided here, as yet. There are a good many reports current respecting the force in which the French are approaching us. Oporto is certainly fallen into their hands, and they are 6 leagues this side of it ; other columns are, it is said, coming by other routes, so that it is very dubious whether we shall stand their attack or not. Our force is given out here to be 16,000 or 17,000 men, but I have good authority that it does not exceed 12,000: if so, I am of opinion we shall embark and leave the French in quiet possession of Lisbon, for I fear we can place but little reliance on the Portuguese fighting.

At the time I was detached up the country Capt. Goldfinch and Lt. Alex. Thomson were ordered to Oporto.* We have heard from Goldfinch, who said the French were very near, and the best hope he had was that of being exchanged soon, when taken. We have heard nothing of him and fear he is either Killed or taken prisoner, but hope it may be otherwise. Had I not been Adjt. I believe I should have gone there too.

Please to give my best love to my dear Mother and all my dear Brothers and sisters, John, Mary, Anna, Ebenezer, Eliza and Margaret. Write me all the news as soon as you can.

Your very loving son,
Rice Jones.

Note I.

This was no solitary experience : nearly every British officer who has penned his reminiscences of the war bears testimony to the courtesy and kindness of the Portuguese. "On entering a town or village," writes the author of *Letters from Portugal and Spain*, "we received from the magistrates billets on the best and richest inhabitants ; and they were obliged not only to admit us, but to furnish us with lodgings for our whole suite. And to do them justice, we have been treated with the courtesy of visitants ; their politeness never allowed us to remember that our quarters had been yielded to a command." Near Coimbra— next to Lisbon, the principal hospital station for the sick and wounded of the British Army, during the war—was a fine Quinta belonging to the Condeça d'A——, where British officers of all ranks were admitted, and received the tenderest care. The wife of a diplomatist, in her interesting *Letters from Lisbon*, penned soon after the war, writes, "How much reason have many of the English to remember the genuine friendship of this family ! I am assured by eye-witnesses that during the war the princely

* Both these young officers were made prisoners by the French on their capture of Oporto, but subsequently effected their escape.

mansion was ever open to our wounded officers ; so much so that the house resembled a hospital, and the lives of several individuals were preserved entirely through the kind and unremitting attention which they received from their really illustrious and excellent hosts." Mark what follows. "I ought not to omit that their example was followed in a more humble way by the peasantry, during the time of that great struggle ; and after this proof of just and grateful feeling, who ought to believe that the Portuguese are incapable of moral regeneration? And yet I hear this asserted every day of my life."

It is, alas! too true that the conduct of the Portuguese Government and many of its incompetent officials during the war, have blinded our eyes to the fine qualities of the Portuguese people, and to the noble conduct of private individuals—the numerous acts of kindness, self-sacrifice and tender sympathy which did so much to alleviate the sufferings of our sick and wounded . . . Even Napier has never allowed one word of acknowledgment of all this to slip from his facile and eloquent pen.

NOTE 2.

INSTRUCTIONS FOR OFFICERS OF THE CORPS OF ROYAL ENGINEERS WHEN ATTACHED TO COLUMNS, OR MOVING THROUGH THE COUNTRY.

The Engineer when moving with a column or otherwise will observe the general features of the country through which they pass, whether hilly, level, woody, open, or enclosed, the state and breadth of the roads, whether they are practicable for artillery, their bearings by Compass, and the Passes and positions in the route. Such parts of the country as may be sufficiently open and level to enable cavalry to act with advantage should be remarked. The Rivers should be particularly attended to, their breadth and depth at the time and place of passing them, and (as far as can be ascertained by enquiry) their state at other seasons of the year should be noted. The bridges, whether of wood or stone, their length and breadth and whether capable of bearing Artillery, or if they could easily be made so should be mentioned. An opinion should be formed of the population of the towns and villages, their distances from each other, and their means of supplying cantonments, provisions, water, and fuel. The situations favourable for encampments should be observed, and whether water, fuel, and materials for hutting are near them. The probability of obtaining mules or draft oxen and carts on the road, should be considered as intimately connected with the movements of troops in this country. In general, whatever can facilitate or retard the march of an army must be carefully attended to, and the whole digested into a written report, accompanied by such sketches as circumstances may admit of. Whenever the army or a column takes a position, the Engineer will make a sketch of the ground upon a scale of 3 in. to a mile, accompanied by explanatory references. Upon arriving at any fortifications or military work, a sketch must be made in the most accurate manner, and in the largest scale the means of the officer will allow, both as to plan and section, accompanied by a general report. They will upon a smaller

13

scale sketch the ground within about 2,000 yards of the place, and will particularly observe if the work be commanded within 1,000 or 1,200 yards of the place, and by references will distinguish such hills as are higher than the place, and how much they appear to be so; the number of troops necessary to defend such work ; the extent of the accommodations and the proportions of it that may be bombproof, the number, size, and construction of the magazines, the supply of water, and the number and nature of the artillery will fall within the report to be made on each work. The nature of the soil, whether favourable or otherwise for sinking trenches and throwing up batteries will naturally be attended to.

(Extract from Official Papers, in Rice Jones' handwriting).

CHAPTER TWO

Sunday, April 9, 1809. " The army commenced their march this day."

Jones, under orders to join Major-General Murray's Brigade, left Lisbon on the 11th, expecting to find it at Torres Vedras :—" It was very dark and wet during the latter part of the ride, and upon my arrival here I was surprised to find no English troops ; I got a billet upon a small house, and found the people very civil." Next morning, he set off for Mafra—hearing that English troops were there, and found his brigade :—" Spent the remainder of the day in viewing the Church, Library, Convent, etc." This wonderful structure—one of John V. extravagances—built to rival the Spanish Escurial, is still one of the chief sights of Portugal. It served a variety of useful purposes during the war.

Next morning, the German Brigade—to which he was attached—consisting of the 1st, 2nd, 5th, and 7th Battalions of the Line, marched to Torres Vedras, where he occupied his former billet. The advance was resumed next day, as far as Obidos, where the division remained seven days :—" The rainy weather still continued ; Lt. Hamilton and myself amused ourselves sketching this place." Jones was now attached to Major-General Tilson's Brigade ; and on April 28th, " The army marched from Caldas ; employed sketching the ground till this day." Here follow detailed and lengthy descriptions of the ground traversed, and of the repairs effected to roads in certain parts, to facilitate the passage of artillery, but as these details are of no interest to the general reader they need not be introduced. The magnificent convent of Alcobaca—of whose kitchen and commissariat arrangements Beckford gives such a delectable account—was reached the same night ; and here ample accommodation would be found for troops and officers ; we know, moreover, from the diary of many a British officer, that a generous hospitality was extended to them by the monks. Jones' diary contains the brief entry, " Dined at the Convent, in which I also slept ; saw the library, Chapel, etc."

The march was resumed next morning, the division, about mid-day passing through the village of Aljubarrota, close to which was fought and won one of the most epoch-marking battles in Portuguese history.

Here, in 1385 the Castilian Army which had invaded Portugal was defeated with great slaughter. Amongst the spoils of victory was the King of Castile's tent, his "travelling Chapel" with all its priceless contents, and an immense bronze cauldron in which the food of the Spanish soldiers had been prepared. The latter—having escaped the devasting effects of Massena's invasion, is still one of the treasured mementos of Alcobaca. Little did the British soldiers who marched through Aljubarrota, on this occasion,—unless, indeed, they were better posted up in Portuguese history than is usually the case— realize that they were treading on classic ground, hallowed by the shedding of British blood in the cause of Portuguese independence, some four hundred years earlier. It was a singular coincidence that, at the crisis referred to, the King of Portugal,—aware how little chance his country, unaided, would have in the struggle with Castile,—had sent post-haste to England for assistance, whence arrived 500 of the famous English archers in time to share in the glorious victory of Aljubarrota. "The English archers," it is recorded, " did yeoman service, and repeated the glories of Crecy and Poitiers." It was to commemorate that great and glorious victory—in which British soldiers played so brilliant a part—that King John I. built the magnificent Convent of Batalha—the "Battle Abbey" of Portugal. And it was in that noble memorial that the Brigade to which Rice Jones was attached passed the night of April 23rd, 1809, he being billeted " upon a small house facing one of the doors of the church, where the people were extremely civil." The glory of Batalha was its Church ; the Refectory and general style of living being on a much humbler scale than at Alcobaca.

The brigade advanced next day to Leyria, where Jones " got an indifferent billet in a house occupied by Staff Surgeons."

Next day, April 25th, 1809, was destined to be ever memorable in the annals of the Peninsular Army, " Sir A. Wellesley is arrived at Lisbon ; Sir J. T. Cradock left this place and the command of the army this morning. Lt.-Col. Fletcher set off for Lisbon in consequence of all heads of Depts. being ordered to meet Sir A. Wellesley there." From this moment a new spirit was instilled into the allied troops ; no further disaster befell them ; strength, discipline, organization, mutual trust, and confidence in their leader increased from day to day, until, after many vicissitudes, but never defeat, four years later, in the glorious campaign of 1813, they drove the last of the invaders from the Peninsula, and on that ever-memorable 10th November, 1813, " the summit of the great Atchubia Mountain just lighted by the rising sun," to quote the inspiring words of the great historian, " fifty thousand men, rushing down its enormous slopes with ringing shouts, seemed to chase the receding shadows into the deep valley. The plains of France, so long overlooked from the towering crags of the Pyrenees, were to be the prize of battle, and the half-famished soldiers in their fury broke through the iron barrier erected by Soult as if it were but a screen of reeds." And the sequel ? Is it not known to every schoolboy ?

The brigade halted at Leyria five days ; here our author fell ill, and though unable to accompany the troops when the advance was resumed, managed to overtake them at Pombal, where, owing to its crowded state, he was unable to obtain a billet, and had to push on to a village near, where " we were quartered in a good house belonging to a lady who seemed rather afraid of us, and frugal." Next morning, though " extremely ill " he accompanied the brigade to Condexa where, through the good offices of some officers of the German Artillery, he got a house " which was a very good one and the people civil." Coimbra was entered next day, May 2nd, " The approach to it, as you descend the hill, along the road from Pombal, is the most beautiful I ever saw, the Rio Mondego being below, having a long stone bridge over it, and the town with its numerous fine Convents on the hills in front." Here Jones was unlucky in his quarters again, " Procured a billet a great way up the hill in a poor house ; slept there, but found myself extremely ill in the morning."

Mafra, April 12, 1809.

My Dear Father,

In my last I informed you of the arrival of Lt.-Col. Fletcher and the other officers. To my great annoyance since that time the army have moved forward, and, in the Brigading our officers, it was the intention to have left me in charge of the works at Lisbon, but fortunately Capt. Chapman heard of it and told Col. F. that it would be very cruel, (as he knew I had made up my mind to be attached to him) to leave me behind, and in consequence of his representations I have just arrived here to relieve Lt. Wedekind of the German Engineers who is to return to Lisbon. You cannot imagine how much I feel obliged to Capt. Chapman for his kindness. I really should have been in a state of despair had I been left. I believe I informed you of my making a Report upon the country I have been reconnoitring ; Capt. Chapman was good enough to assist me with his advice and opinion in drawing it up, and I understand the Commander in-Chief was pleased with it. I am, for the present, attached to Maj.-Gen. Murray's Brigade consisting of the German Legion which forms the Advanced Body of the left wing of the Army ; but I have applied to be appointed to the Brigade of cavalry, under Maj.-Gen. Cotton ; and this I have done for two reasons ; the first is that I intend to make use of Sir W. W. Wynn's name when I see the General, and the other is that I think I shall like the active service of a Dragoon Brigade. The Brigade I belong to marches to-morrow morning to Torres Vedras, and from thence to Obidos and Leyria. . . .

It is now generally understood that an engagement will certainly take place previous to our evacuating Portugal. Whatever may be the result I shall certainly endeavour, as well as the rest of the Army, to do my duty as a good soldier. My servant turns out very well indeed and is of very

17

great service to me.   I have been obliged to get another horse for him
and my baggage, for which I gave 90 dollars, but he is so poor I am
dubious of his standing the campaign.   All my baggage is once more
afloat; we are ordered to embark it in the *Britannia*, No. 92, where it is
now deposited, and I only have a blanket and portmanteau with me, besides
the valise I carry behind at all times.

We are all quartered in an immense palace here, belonging to the
Kings of Portugal; it is so large that although there are seven Regiments
now in it, it appears capable of holding several more; it is also very
grand and beautifully situated.   .   .   .

I remain your most loving son,
RICE JONES.

LEYRIA, *April* 24, 1809.

MY DEAR FATHER,

I have just arrived here.   I wrote to you on the 12th inst. from Mafra,
since that we have marched to Obidos where we halted a week, and
where I was removed from M.-Genl. Murray's Brigade to M.-Genl.
Tilson's.   I liked Gen. Murray very much the little time I was with
him, and Genl. Tilson is very civil and kind to me; I accompany him
the whole of the march; this is all I have to do with him as yet.   We
marched on the 22nd inst. from Obidos to Alcobaca, and proceeded to
Batalha yesterday; we this day marched into Leyria which is at present
the Head Qrs. of the army and is uncommonly full of troops; all the
army being here except Genl. Murray's Division and   .   .   .   You
have no idea of the difficulty there is to procure quarters and provisions
at the different places we march through; very little or nothing is to be
purchased after a Brigade has occupied a town a day or so, and we are
obliged to depend upon the Commissariat issuing the rations we are
allowed, but which it is often impossible to get, particularly forage for
the horses; however my horses both get on extremely well, and if we
halt here a day or two (which I rather think we shall) they will be quite
fresh again.

My servant turns out very well; he is not yet quite up to foraging and
buying provisions when they are scarce, but I daresay he will improve.
.   .   .   It certainly would have been as well if I had seen Genl. Beresford,
but I thought it would appear forward or impudent to call often upon
him; he is now a Field Marshal in the Portuguese Service, and a great
number of officers have got rank along with him; however I am not
ambitious of their honours, and would much rather serve with my own
Brigade in Action than with them; indeed I should certainly have
declined any of his appointments had they been offered to me.   I understand that Sir A. Wellesley is arrived at Lisbon; I suppose that will cause
a new arrangement of the army, if not new measures.   We are quite
ignorant of our intended operations, but imagine we are to advance
towards the French.   The following is the disposition of the army.   (Full
particulars are here given).   .   .   .

We are now nearly 100 miles from Lisbon on the way to Oporto.   This
is a city and the largest place we have seen since Lisbon.   .   .   .

I am particularly well in health, notwithstanding we march very early (in general about 4 o'clock) and it is seldom we can get breakfast—tea or milk, butter or cheese, it is useless to expect.

Your loving son,
RICE JONES.

ADDRESSED TO:—

    CAPT. R. JONES,

        ROYAL DENBIGH MILITIA,

            STRATFORD COFFEE HOUSE, OXFORD STREET, LONDON.

For the stirring events of the next few days, we must turn to other sources for information. Our diarist is no Boswell; he indulges neither in gossip, nor in criticism of his superiors—as was so much the fashion in the Peninsular Army. Nor does he take one behind the scenes. Apart from this, he was laid up with illness during the stay of the army at Coimbra, and unable to take part in any functions, military or social. The only entries of interest are as follows:—" May 2, Sir A. Wellesley arrived here this morning: May 3, Marshal Beresford arrived; May 5, Maj.-Gen. Tilson's Brigade marched for Viseu, I was too ill to accompany them; Lt. Boothby took my place. Mr. Fitzpatrick pronounced my disorder as ague and ordered me Bark."

Sir Arthur Wellesley having been selected for the command of the army destined to drive the French out of North Portugal, the troops were ordered to assemble at Coimbra; the British regiments as they marched in, meeting with a most enthusiastic reception from the inhabitants; their advent "being announced," wrote an eyewitness, " by a ringing of bells which brought out crowds of people who lined the roads, bridge, and the streets of the city, receiving us with vivas and huzzas; the soldiers, as they passed, being covered with flowers, showered down from all the windows which were thronged with senhoras." At night, a grand illumination took place, which was repeated every night during the stay of the army. " And with every inducement to tempt us out; the streets being graced with a charming supply of Bonitas Senhoras, who professed 'gustar muitos os Officiales Ingleses bonitos,' (to be greatly pleased with the handsome English officers) we were, indeed, so cordially received and delightfully entertained, that it can hardly be called vanity to say we believed them in earnest."

Popular enthusiasm reached a climax on the 7th of May, when the army was reviewed by the Commander-in-Chief, on a sandy plain near the city; and an eyewitness wrote "a most imposing and magnificent spectacle it presented." The troops formed a line extending for over two miles; and when, after receiving the General, the regiments wheeled into column and marched past, " the excitement and enthusiasm of the spectators knew no bounds; the speedy and final deliverance of their country from the French being looked forward to with the utmost confidence."

Lord Londonderry, an officer on the Headquarter Staff declared that, "to some of the troops which stood that day under arms, it is not going too far to affirm, that the whole world can produce none superior"; and he singled out for special commendation, the Brigade of Guards, the 29th and 83rd Regiments, and the four battalions of the King's German Legion, and he went on to state that the whole were in "the highest state of discipline and efficiency, and all appeared animated by one spirit—an ardent desire to meet the enemy."

A feature of this display, which attracted little attention at the time, and the enormous significance of which escaped the notice of nearly everyone present, was the appearance for the first time, in line with British troops, of the newly-raised Portuguese battalions, under British officers. Who, indeed, at that moment would have dared to foretell of these raw, half-disciplined, mean-looking recruits, the glorious part they were destined to play in the future liberation of the Peninsula ? "It was impossible not to be forcibly struck with the superiority of the English over the Portuguese soldiers in external appearance," wrote Lord Londonderry, in comparing the two ; adding, however, that "the latter seemed to be inferior specimens of their nation, being diminutive and narrow-chested in the extreme ; yet were they extremely steady under arms." In justice to the Portuguese soldiers who cut such a poor figure, I would recall a circumstance which was probably unknown to the distinguished critic, and is habitually ignored by British writers, namely, that the cream of the Portuguese Army had been skimmed off by Marshal Junot, after his seizure of the country, two years previously, and these men, in accordance with Napoleon's invariable custom, were sent off to fight his battles in other lands, some even surviving to oppose us at Waterloo. Several of the Portuguese officers, to the eternal disgrace of their cloth, enrolled themselves under the Republican banner of France, and subsequently accompanied Massena, in the capacity of advisers, during his invasion of their country in 1810-11.

During the stay of the army at Coimbra, provisions were abundant, and, contrary to expectation, "the inhabitants supplied every article at a moderate price." Would that this noble example had been copied on certain notable occasions, in modern times ! The enormous expense of supporting the army may be gathered from the statement, on reliable authority, that the British troops, alone, circulated in Coimbra a sum of not less than £10,000 a day ; while the money spent by the entire army exceeded £100,000 per week ; practically the whole of which was defrayed out of the British Exchequer.

The day after the troops had been reviewed by their new commander, was commenced the advance which reached its climax at

Oporto five days later, in that brilliant feat of arms commemorated in the title of the Duke of Wellington's eldest son—Lord Douro, followed by the expulsion of the French from North Portugal. The exultation with which news of the victory was received at Coimbra may readily be conceived. But had any one of the inhabitants of that proud and ancient seat of learning, whose towers were haunted by a thousand memories, at this moment of delirious rejoicing, been vouchsafed a peep into futurity, and venture to disclose his vision, like a modern Jeremiah, he would have been relegated forthwith to the Mondego, or an asylum.

Poor Jones was not fit to move before the 9th, when he rejoined his brigade, but "was unable to make any observations on this part of the country in consequence of illness." He was, however, sufficiently recovered to be able to be in the saddle at 2 o'clock next morning, and to accompany his Chief, Lieut.-Colonel Fletcher, on a long day's work, in course of which, news reached them that the army was in contact with the enemy; and towards evening, they passed over the ground from which the French had just been dislodged; and later, caught sight of the enemy retiring along the road to Oporto. The troops were halted; Colonel Fletcher and his party returning to Bemposta, near Pinheiro, where Headquarters were for the night. "I find myself nearly recovered now" is the final entry for the day. No tonic so good as a brush with the enemy!

An English traveller passing over the same ground, a few years later, tells us how he was shown " with pride the bed-room in which Wellington slept," in the Quinta of Meelhadas, on the night in question, and the very "log of wood in the courtyard upon which our hero, who had reached the Quinta before preparations could be completed for his reception, was found asleep, wrapped in his military cloak."

May 11th. "Rose early and rode with Lt.-Col. Fletcher to Oliviera where we waited until Sir A. Wellesley's arrival; we then accompanied him with the advance until about $\frac{1}{4}$ mile from Grijo, when we perceived a body of the enemy's cavalry on a hill close to the road at a little distance from us. Our cavalry formed ready to charge, and our light troops commenced firing with those of the enemy that were in a wood which concealed the village and the French line. General Stewart's Brigade advanced also, and upon bringing up a gun the French cavalry retired immediately. The 16th Portuguese Regiment then turned their right flank, whilst M.-Genl. Murray's Brigade attacked their left and obliged them to retreat with precipitation. As soon as they had descended a hill on which they had encamped our cavalry charged them to Carvalhos, whilst our artillery played upon them from the hill. I was with Sir Arthur's suite this day." Headquarters were at the Convent of Grijal this night.

May 12th. " Rode this morning early to Carvalhos where we heard the enemy had retired across the Douro during the night, and had blown up the bridge of boats across the river at Villa Nova. I was then ordered with Capt. Burgoyne, R.E., and a squadron of the 14th Light Dragoons, and the 2nd Battalion of the King's German Legion to the village of Vintos, in order to collect boats for the passage of the troops across the river. I proceeded with Capt. B. to the ferry above the village, where we found it was easy to procure boats. Capt. B. therefore directed me to rejoin the army and report to Col. Fletcher. I took the road to Villa Nova, and upon arriving at the Convent in that place, found Col. Fletcher with Sir A. Wellesley in a redoubt which had been evacuated by the enemy. I reported the state of affairs at Vintos and remained with them for some time, during which I observed the French retiring from Oporto, but their guards and sentries very quiet at their posts. A few boats then crossed the Douro to us, and General Hill's Brigade began to go over in them ; as soon as they landed they marched up a steep hill and took possession of a large unfinished building. The French perceiving this marched down towards them in column, their light troops being posted behind the walls and in the gardens all round ; the former were soon checked by the fire of some guns we had brought to the spot where Sir A. and we remained ; while the latter were at length and with some difficulty dislodged. M.-Genl. Murray having now arrived with his brigade from Vintos, and Major-Gen. Sherbrooke with the Guards, and B.-Genl. Stewart's Brigade having crossed the river below, the enemy retreated immediately, and our cavalry charging them brought in many prisoners and left a number on the field. I crossed the river with Genl. Stewart's Brigade." A bed was found that night at Genl. Howorth's quarters.

The only entry of interest, next day, is that Colonel Fletcher had nearly completed a new bridge across the river, by the evening, to replace the bridge of boats destroyed by the French ; " it was very wet all day." Next day, May 14th, Jones was ordered by Sir A. Wellesley to join Major-General Hill's Brigade, which he accompanied to Braga. Continuing the advance on the 17th, orders were received to return to Braga, which was reached again the same evening. Here, it was " reported that the French had dispersed, and our army was returning." Our author took no further part in pursuing the French over the border,—in which famous retreat they shed nearly everything but the clothes they stood in.

During the late fighting, two Engineer officers had been captured by the enemy, " May 19th, Lt. W. Thomson who has escaped from the French during their retreat, arrived, and dined with me." And next day, " Col. Fletcher arrived here with Capt. Goldfinch who has been fortunate enough to make his escape from the French."

Next day, May 21st, Jones returned to Oporto; May 23rd, "Employed all this day drawing a plan of the ground where we passed the Douro on the 12th. Went to the Opera in the evening with Col. Fletcher. I was this day very ill; rather better at night."

OPORTO, May 13th, 1809.

MY DEAR FATHER,

I have only time to let you know that thro' divine Mercy I have escaped unhurt during all the late severe but glorious affairs we have had with the enemy. Soon after writing to you from Leyria, I was taken very ill with an ague which I suppose I had brought from the coast of Essex; and at Coimbra, where the army halted, I was so bad that when M.-Genl. Tilson's Brigade, to which I was attached, was ordered on a service by itself, I was unable to accompany it. However when the army moved I persevered in accompanying them and very providentially recovered the very first day's march, and am now as well as ever I was in my life. Sir A. Wellesley's Dispatches will inform you more of the affairs than I have time to do. On the 9th instant we marched from Coimbra; on the next morning we fell in with and drove in their advanced post about 9 miles, and took their position at Oliviera. I was a little in the rear during this business, but came up in time to see the enemy retire from ground they had occupied about 400 yards in front of us. On the 11th instant after marching some distance we found them posted very advantageously at Greija, but in a little time we turned both flanks, and they retreated precipitately. I was near Sir Arthur all the day, and it was certainly a very fine sight, but was far exceeded by the passage of the Douro yesterday, and the defeat of the French at this place, which was as gallant a thing as was ever done: I was with the artillery cannonading them from the other side of the river at the commencement, and afterwards crossed with the 29th Regt. and B.-Genl. Stewart in time to make them scamper off. I have great reason to be thankful for my preservation.   .   .

Poor Hamilton of our Corps was very badly wounded yesterday; I understand a musquet ball entered one of his thighs and lodged in the other; the ball is extracted; I am now endeavouring to find him, to render him what assistance I can.   .   .   .

Your very loving son,
RICE JONES.

OPORTO, May 22nd, 1809.

MY DEAR FATHER,

You must allow me again to write you a very hurried epistle; in fact we seldom hear of an opportunity of writing to England until a short time before the letters are sent; however I always write a letter if possible. I have just been favoured with yours which I was very happy at receiving. I wrote to you from hence the day after we took this place; the next day the whole army marched, and after pursuing the enemy as far as the borders of Spain through a country that they had burnt and destroyed wherever they could, and where it was impossible to procure any provisions or forage (the inhabitants having all quitted their houses, most of which the French burnt) we have given up the pursuit, and great part of the troops are returned here, whilst the rest are returning as fast as they can. I believe we begin to move back again towards Lisbon to-morrow, in consequence of a French force having marched for that place under Marshal Victor; and it is said that we shall probably enter Spain as soon as we have beaten his army.

We are rather disappointed at our not having taken Marshal Soult and the whole of his army, but however, his troops are in a very distressed and scattered state, and certainly had a complete run for the narrow escape they have had; they have gone into Galicia and the force they have got off with are by some people estimated at 8,000 men; they have blown up great quantities of their ammunition, left great part of their guns, and an immense number of horses all along the road, some killed and others wounded, etc.; they have also lost great part of their baggage, and even left some of their knapsacks and kits about the roads.

Ever since the passage of the Douro on the 12th instant (which was a most daring, and as it turned out, most glorious attempt, and which the French all own they had not the most distant idea we should try to do, as they had destroyed the bridge) I have been attached to M.-Genl. Hill's Brigade, instead of Lieut. Williams who was left here ill, but who is now well and has relieved me. We marched from here on the road to Ponte de Lima for two days, when we received an order to join the rest of the army on the road to Braga: this turning out of one road into the other, threw our brigade into the rear, but which turned out rather fortunate than otherwise, as we did not advance so far in the country the French have destroyed, and consequently did not suffer so much as the rest of the army. Genl. Hill is a very good kind of man. I lived at his table during the time we were on the march, when it was impossible to get anything to eat elsewhere, and slept in the same empty houses along with his staff. Genl. Tilson's Brigade was at Chaves the other day. I expect to join them as soon as we can ascertain the way they are going; in the meantime I am with Col. Fletcher at Hd. Qrs., detached about in all directions, whenever a Brigade wants an Engineer with them. The Colonel is a very good man; he was particularly kind and attentive to me during my late illness, as were all our officers; Capt. Burgoyne removed me into his own quarters at Coimbra, and rendered me every little assistance which a sick person required. I am now getting quite strong again, and feel as well as ever I was in my life, thank God;—notwithstanding we have had a great deal of rain all the time we were marching after the French, and in general were obliged to sleep in our wet cloaks, etc. It is now very fine weather again. I should like to know what the people in England think of our attack of this place, as well as our other operations; I assure you we think it altogether a very gallant affair.   .   .   .   Capt. Goldfinch and Lt. Thomson are here, they escaped from the French during the confusion of their precipitate retreat and are very well.   .   .   .

Your loving son,
RICE JONES.

P.S.—I assure you my losing the adjutancy had not any tendency whatever to make me uncomfortable; I believe I resigned it with as good a
grace as most people would have done. I am only anxious to continue
with the troops that keep the field, as I am very much afraid of being left
in some garrison town; I have hitherto escaped, but had some near
chances for it. My sickness was so far fortunate as it prevented my
being detached with Genl. Tilson's Brigade which has not been in
action, and perhaps also from being sent back to Lisbon with Capt.
Chapman from Coimbra; he made every effort to remain with the army
but could not. I have now made up my mind to be perfectly satisfied
with whatever occurs, or as the French prisoners say, with the *Fortune de
la Guerre.* My best horse stands the campaign very well, the other's
back is very sore, I fear I shall be obliged to get another here until he
gets well, altho' I cannot afford it. I am quite delighted at having been
in all our actions; I am now beginning to be used to the whizzing of the
bullets about one, which at first was not very agreeable, altho' everyone
of course took it quietly.

The following interesting sketch of Wellington, during the pursuit
of Soult's Army, is supplied by a Portuguese gentleman :—"I was a
boy then, living at Salamonde. I recollect seeing the first two
soldiers of the British Army who entered the city. They were two
dragoons with carbines in their hands, who rode up the street without
uttering a word to any one, and then halted like two statues. Soon
after, others followed; and I cannot express to you the joy of our
hearts—the enthusiasm with which your countrymen were received.
My father, who spoke English perfectly, had received notice that
Sir Arthur Wellesley would take up his quarters in his house, and
dinner was prepared accordingly. It was towards evening, and I was
with my father, when an officer wrapped in a large cloak entered the
saloon, and told him that he had come to remain there. "I regret,"
said my father, "that I cannot give you the best accommodation my
house affords, as the General is coming here himself." "I am the
General," said the officer; and for the first time I saw your great
Duke. Throwing off his cloak, and an orderly bringing in a case of
maps, he desired my father to accompany him into an inner room,
and there, for two hours did they sit looking over them, while my
father was describing the country. During all this time dinner was
waiting; but not a particle of food would the General touch till he
had formed his plans. The following morning the army again
marched in pursuit of the French."

The extreme difficulty of supplying the troops with food during the
pursuit may be gathered from Wellington's General Orders; thus,
under date May 17th, 1809 :—"The troops will have observed the
extreme difficulty of supplying them with bread in this part of the
country. . . . Till the army be in a more plentiful country the
allowance of bread is to be one pound, and one pound and a half of

meat each man. . . . When bread cannot be delivered to the troops, they must have two pounds of beef for their ration." Short commons, as is invariably the case, brought demoralization in its train, and drew from the Bishop of Braga, who seems to have assumed the *rôle*, for the nonce of Commissariat Officer—the following mild protest :— "I likewise avail myself of this opportunity to inform your Excellency that, notwithstanding my endeavours that supplies of provisions of all kinds should be brought forward at this place for the use of the army under your command, I have not succeeded until now to that extent that I promised to do, on account of the arbitrary manner in which the provisions are taken possession of at this place by the different soldiers of your Excellency's army, etc., etc."

Another difficulty Wellington had to contend with was the improvidence of his troops, who, when entrusted with three days' rations, in advance, would consume the whole at a sitting, "from want of attention to this, and care of their bread, the best operations are necessarily relinquished." With a view to the prevention of the practice, orders were issued for the men's bread to be inspected twice a day.

On the return of the army to Coimbra, the Commander of the Forces issued the following stinging rebuke. " Not only have outrages been committed by whole corps, but there is no description of property of which the unfortunate inhabitants of Portugal have not been plundered by the British soldiers, whom they have received into their houses ; or by stragglers from the different regiments of the army." And after describing the disciplinary measures rendered necessary by these disgraceful proceedings, the Commander of the Forces goes on to state that, "The people of Portugal deserve well of the army : they have in every instance treated the soldiers well ; and there never was an army so well supplied, or which had so little excuse for plunder."

The sequel to this disastrous retreat is thus described by Capt. Charles Boothby, who was made acquainted with the facts by an intelligent French officer :—Marshal Soult, after he had effected his retreat from Portugal, immediately repaired to the quarters of Marshal Ney, at Lugo, and was ushered in by the officer above-mentioned, who, from the ante-room could distinctly over-hear the altercation that ensued. Soult on entering the room where Ney was, went forward with open arms to embrace him.

"Stand back," said Ney, "I don't know you, where do you come from ? You come flying, like a coward, from the enemies of the Emperor."

"Allons donc," returned Soult. " I come to save Lugo, which you were on the point of losing."

"I neither want assistance," said the other, "nor are you in a condition to give me any. I have been met by hundreds of your

straggling fugitives. They all had abandoned their arms, that they
might fly the faster; but their packs, heavy with plunder, were
religiously preserved! It is you, Monsieur le Maréchal, who have
taught them to throw away their muskets in order that they might
carry the more booty, when your orderly-book gave up such a town
as Oporto to a three days' pillage. Is that the way, sir, you consult
your master's interests? To give up the second city of the country,
you take in his name, to the horrible excesses of your brutal soldiers!
You are no longer a Marshal of France. I will no longer acknowledge you as a chief in authority under the Emperor."

Ney, at length, became so grossly abusive that Soult, unable any
longer to command his temper, used some expressions which so
infuriated Ney that suddenly drawing his sword, he said, " Villain,
defend thyself"—a mandate which was instantly obeyed; and the
furious combatants were only, at last separated by General Mathieu
rushing into the room. Meanwhile the quarrel had extended to the
troops commanded by the respective Marshals, who had commenced
firing at each other; and it was only by the personal intervention of
their chiefs that the affray was stopped.

Headquarters having quitted Oporto on May 24th, Jones was
ordered to reconnoitre the river Tamega from Chaves to the Douro;
" but was prevented by illness and the advice of Surgeon Fitzpatrick;
I still continued very ill indeed." The arduous duties of a campaign
must have been trying to a young man who had just risen from a
sick bed; and when on top of all this we come across such an entry
as " arrived in the dark, and very wet; slept in my wet cloak, having
waited in vain for my servant, until late," it is no wonder he was
knocked over again, so soon. His brother officers had all gone with
the army. " I am now quite alone and very unwell; consequently have
little to do or write." Two days later, " Rode to Mr. Fitzpatrick's;
I am considerably better than yesterday; continue taking quantities
of Bark." Many a man would have grumbled at the hard luck which
kept him in the rear, in such stirring times; but he writes;—May
28th. " The end of this day has nearly completed my 21st year, and
therefore I shall begin a new book, hoping that when I arrive at the
end of another I may have as much reason for thankfulness to God
for his Providence as I have at present."

(Signed) RICE JONES.

Convalescence went on steadily; he was soon able to walk about
the city; bought Lalande's *Tables of Logarithms*, and obtained the
loan, from a wounded brother officer of *Zimmerman on Solitude*.

May 31st. " Rode with General Howorth and Surgeon Fitzpatrick
over the ground of the action on the 12th; then crossed the bridge
to Villa Nova, and visited the spot from whence we cannonaded the
enemy on that day. NOTE.—We had four guns on the old French

work and one more, to the left. This was a very fine day, and the views of the city and river were delightful."

The operations pertaining to the passage of the Douro have been so fully described in various histories, that it is needless to recapitulate them here. It may be of interest to state, however, that, with the exception of the ground immediately adjoining the famous Convent whence Sir Arthur directed the operations on that memorable occasion, which was a good deal cut up for purposes of defence during the subsequent Civil Wars,--the river banks and the unfinished building which our troops seized and held after crossing, are but little changed since the eventful day in question.

Sunday, the 4th of June, finds our author once more on the march, after the army. "I rode a pony I have bought from Burgoyne for 60 dollars, and my large horse carried my baggage; the other's back being sore. In the afternoon it rained very fast. I halted here (St. Joao de Madeira) and got a billet upon a good house near the Church where I was used very well." Here follow as usual detailed descriptions of the ground traversed, from day to day, June 6th, he reached Coimbra. "Quartered in a poor house in Rua do Corpo Santo, and found to my surprise that Sir A. Wellesley had proceeded towards Abrantes." . Setting off, in pursuit of Headquarters, on the 8th, with a friend, they called at the Quinta da Bouca,—"where we were very hospitably received by the Fidalgo who resided there, and who directed us the nearest road to Venda das Figueras." They halted for the night at Almofalla, "where I was taken by the Capitao Mor into his own house and was very well treated."

CHAPTER THREE

May 31st (contd.). Thomar was reached next night, where they were billeted on a very good house; and Abrantes the following day, June 10th :—"Where I found Col. Fletcher, Boothby, Burgoyne, etc." Here he remained till the 25th, losing his baggage horse, which had to be shot.

ABRANTES, June 17th, 1809.

MY DEAR FATHER,

I wrote to you from Oporto, upon our return to that place; since that time nothing material has occurred. We marched from Oporto to Coimbra and from thence to this town, in the neighbourhood of which all the army are now hutted or encamped, and where Sir A. Wellesley is with Head Qrs. All our officers are now here with Col. Fletcher, making plans, etc. . . .

I understand that Capt. Buchanan is Adjutant vice Jones resigned, notwithstanding what I was promised on that subject; it however gives me little concern, as I had not placed much confidence in it, and indeed am not very anxious about it; yet I think Handfield should let you or me know something more about the affair, for you know his promises were very decided, even in the name of the General. I am certainly very unfortunate in these things. I have had the misfortune to lose my baggage horse for which I gave 90 dollars, when we marched from Lisbon; he died a day or two ago; he was a good deal knocked up during the marches and at last died. If he had been killed or glandered I should have been allowed £18 for him, but as it now happens I shall get nothing. I must do as well as I can to get another before we march from here, but the expenses of this kind will ruin me if it goes on. Notwithstanding these untoward circumstances I feel happy and thankful that my health has been restored and continued to me; I hope it will please God to continue that blessing, and I shall then be able to get through this world somehow or other. . . .

This is a large town upon the river Tagus which runs to Lisbon, about 100 miles from here; it is one of the places I was sent to reconnoitre when I first came to this country. It is said that we are to move into Spain shortly; part of the army is advanced towards the frontiers. On the 10th instant the French endeavoured to force the Bridge of Alcantara, a town in Spain about 50 or 60 miles off, upon the river Tagus; our people blew up the bridge by a mine which Lt. Stanway of our Corps had prepared, and which, luckily for him succeeded; soon afterwards they retired, but I do not know where they are.

M.-Genl. Tilson whom I was attached to returns to England; he could not agree with Marshal Beresford, and was disgusted at being obliged to serve among the Portuguese troops. Capt. Chapman continues at Lisbon still; they are fortifying it upon a large scale; this also is to be fortified, Capt. Patton has been here some time for that purpose.

I hope you will let me know whatever news you have, particularly what B.-Major Handfield says; I really think he has not been long enough in office to entitle him to forget every promise he makes; however you may remember me to him when you see him. You should get a map of Spain and Portugal in order to trace our movements; for if we go into Spain I daresay we shall not be idle. I shall have to resume the study of Spanish, I have my grammar, etc., with me. I get on tolerably well with Portuguese, at least I can make them understand almost anything I wish, yet I have not studied much, thinking we shall soon have occasion for Spanish. In fact I neither like Portuguese nor Portugal, although the country and climate is fine. . . .

On the 29th of May I was 21 years of age; I did not fail to send you all my best wishes, which is the only thing a poor soldier could do (upon a march) when he became of age. Whenever you write give my best love to my dear mother and all my dear brothers and sisters. . . . Tell my dear mother I would write to her as well as you, was I not fearful of the expense of postage; she may be assured I do not want in inclination.   I remain, etc., etc.,

RICE JONES.

Capt. Burgoyne and another officer having been sent off to reconnoitre the northern frontier of Portugal,—"Lt.-Col. Fletcher wished me to reconnoitre the river Zezere, but I was unable to do so for want of horses."

June 25th. "The Col. having desired me to proceed to reconnoitre some rivers in Spain," a start was made, in company with Col. Delancy and Lt. D., of the Portuguese Engineers. Passing through Castello-Branco and Salvaterra, they entered Spain, for the first time, paying a visit to Sir R. Wilson and the Lusitanian Legion. Next day, June 29th, "Rode to Alcantara with Lt. Stanway to see the bridge he has destroyed; the second arch from the right bank is blown up, and not a stone of the arch is standing. The arch which is destroyed was blown up and re-built by Charles V., of Spain."

This magnificent bridge—one of the finest specimens of Roman work in the Peninsula, if not in the world, was built across the Tagus, A.D. 105, by the Emperor Trajan. The material is granite, laid in large blocks; no mortar being used in its construction. Its length is 616 ft. with a width of 20 ft. The two middle piers are of a height of 190 ft.; the arch having a span of 150 ft. In the centre of the bridge is a Triumphal Arch bearing a Latin inscription. In the Journals of General Sir A. Dickson, Royal Artillery (edited by Major J. Leslie, R.A.), we learn that the bridge was broken by order of Colonel Mayne, of the Lusitanian Legion; that the Spaniards were very angry, as it was subsequently ascertained that only a small body of cavalry were approaching; they said the bridge had been preserved by the Goths, Moors, and other barbarous nations, and at last destroyed by the Portuguese—the most barbarous of all. As a matter of fact, this piece of vandalism was performed by an Englishman, Lieut. Stanway, of the Engineers, by superior orders.

Placencia, July 2nd. "This morning I received a message from the Junta, saying they wished to see me; upon my going there with Capt. Whittingham (who is a Brigadier-General in the Spanish Service), they requested me to fix upon a spot the most proper for a bridge over the river Teitar; this I promised to do, and they gave me an order for the different villages near to do whatever I required for the service." Proceeding on his mission, our author found himself billeted one night "upon the house of a very well-disposed peasant"; the next "on the house of a cross old widow woman." Reaching Soto Serrano, very late, the night following, "we had to awaken the Alcadi who afterwards had to awaken his Secretario, and after holding a council with him he endeavoured to waken the people of several houses, but for some time in vain; at last we were received into a house, got some supper and then repaired to a clean, good bed."

On the return journey, he passed through Villar, "found here some Spanish troops; the officers were civil and I got good accommodation." Next day he regained Placencia, where he was joined by Colonel Fletcher, and remained there till July 15th, drawing up a report of his late proceedings. On the latter date, he set off, in accordance with orders, to reconnoitre the river Teitar. At Losar he found Sir R. Wilson, with whom he took up his quarters, "and during all the time lived at his table." Next day, July 18th, he accompanied Sir R. Wilson and his cavalry to Arenas, where a visit was paid to the fine palace of the Infant Don Luis which had been given to Godoy,—"and we got the acclamations of the populace."

"Next day Sir R. Wilson and myself rode to the Bridge of Teitar, and returned; he posted his troops in their position."

PLASENCIA, July 11, 1809.

MY DEAR FATHER, . . . On the 27th ult. the army marched from Abrantes and arrived here on the 8th instant. Sir Arthur is gone to the Spanish Army under Genl. Cuesta who are on the Tagus at Puente del Arzobispo and we are now halting until his return; the advance has this instant been ordered to march and it is supposed we shall all follow to-morrow morning. The French Army under Victor are at Talavera Veija about four or five days march from us, but is uncertain where or whether they will wait for us at all. I was sent forward from Abrantes on the 26th to reconnoitre the country about the rivers Alagon (which we have already crossed) and the Tietar which we shall cross about 15 miles from hence. When I arrived here I found the French had left this place just a week; their outposts had never entered this city although they had been in sight of it some time. They have as usual burnt and destroyed all the bridges, towns, etc., on their retreat.

31

During the whole of the march the army have been encamped in huts, so that I was fortunate in being sent alone in front, as I always got in the best quarters, being the only British officer they had then seen. I am considered as attached to the 4th Division of the army, but I have not yet joined them and we expect a new arrangement when B.-Genl. Craufurd with the light troops from England come up; they are barely two or three days march behind. . . . The Colonel has made me an offer of the Adjutancy when vacant which I told him I should accept with pleasure. . . . In the meantime he desired me to be with Mulcaster in order to see his method of carrying on the service. This will give me three shillings a day more pay, and is most probably a more permanent situation than most other Adjutants; besides which I shall be with the Col. at Hd. Qrs. of the army always.

I have bought another horse for 60 dollars, but it is a poor-looking beast; however he will do very well to carry my servant and baggage. My large horse is very much out of condition and has rather a sore back; I mean to give him all the rest possible until the time when we are likely to have an action, and then I shall mount him. How does my old friend Hollyhock go on? he would be invaluable in this country; you cannot imagine the superiority of the English horses; I will certainly never leave England again without one. You know very well that on service the greatest cares and troubles of mounted officers are their horses. . . . I hope you will continue to send me all the news you can; nothing gives one so much pleasure as receiving a letter from you. . . . My love waits on my dear mother, my dear brothers and sisters. . . .

RICE JONES.

Great events were impending. The British Army was advancing, and a few days later would be engaged with the enemy at Talavera. Napier, in his history of the war, tells us that "Wilson, ascending the right bank of the Teitar, gained the pass of Arenas and the pass of San Pedro Bernado in which position, having 4,000 troops, he covered the rich Vera de Plascencia and menaced Victor's communication with the King."

To continue the diary :—"*July 20th.* At 4 o'clock this morning I set off from Arenas with my servant and a guide, until we arrived a short distance from Parillas, where we were informed that a party of 40 French Dragoons had just entered that village which they were then plundering; we therefore turned to the right towards Naval Carno which place we were also prevented entering by hearing that 13 of the enemy's cavalry had just arrived there. Presently we found some German Dragoons, and proceeded quietly to Oropesa. Upon my arrival I saw Sir A. Wellesley and delivered him some messages from Sir R. Wilson. I was soon ordered to be in readiness to return to Sir R. Wilson to-night."

This very day the British Army had reached Oropesa, having crossed the Teitar two days previously ;—"An English officer of the Staff-corps,"—says Napier, "having taken the materials of an old house, felled some pine trees three miles off, and in one day thrown a solid bridge over that river."

July 21st. "At 11 o'clock last night I set out with my servant and a guide, and having an order to take a Spanish escort of cavalry with me from—(?), I left my horse there to return with my servant to the army, and mounted on a Spanish Dragoon horse, and accompanied by one Dragoon I rode to Naval Carno where I procured another horse, an escort of 19 men and a guide, and proceeded towards Buenventura hoping to find Sir R. Wilson there. At Hontares near the Puento de Teitar, a party of French Dragoons commenced firing upon us which we were unable to return for want of ammunition, but upon our proceeding to charge they retired up the hills, on the other side of which they were supported by a patrole of cavalry ; we therefore thought it prudent to give up the pursuit of them, and continued on the bank of the Teitar to Buenventura ; at this place I left the corporal and eight of the men, their horses being unable to proceed, and with the remaining ten men I followed Sir R. Wilson who had left that place in the morning. Soon after leaving the town I learnt that the enemy were in Navalmorguerde, and I therefore sent orders for the party at Buenventura to continue their route after Sir R. Wilson's troops, as far as they were able. I overtook Sir R. Wilson on his march, and he soon after took a direction towards the Teitar on the banks of which he encamped, near Ladrada. I dined with him, and slept there."

July 22. Left Ladrada at daylight, at a distance of 2 leagues found the corporal and his party of Spanish cavalry, halted and got a cup of chocolate, and taking with me 10 Dragoons ascended a steep hill to Navalmorguarde, where we were received with the greatest enthusiasm. Hearing that firing had been heard all the morning in the direction of Gamonal, I made the best of my way towards that town, avoiding the villages occupied by the enemy, and rode as fast as I could towards Talavera, which the British and Spaniards were then entering. I had the greatest difficulty before I could pass the Spanish column, but at length joined the army once more. I procured a billet, but altho' I walked about to find my servant and horses until dark I was obliged to retire to rest without either.

Talavera, Sunday, July 23rd. At dawn of day I walked over the British camp, but was some hours before I could find my servant, etc. I immediately mounted my horse, in order to find Col. Fletcher who has appointed me his Adjutant. I joined the column in advance expecting that he would soon arrive there, but hearing that he was with Sir A. Wellesley near the bridge over the Alberche, I proceeded there where I found him at a conference between Sir Arthur and Cuesta ; reconnoitred the banks of the river with the Col., and was just beginning to act with Lord Macduff, Wittingham, etc., when Sir Arthur mounted and I was obliged to follow him ; he rode towards the army and ordered them to return to the ground they had occupied during the night, the intended attack being postponed until next day.

Monday, July 24. "At 2 o'clock this morning part of the line began their march towards the River, where they arrived about half past 4 o'clock, and were surprised to find that the enemy had left their position—(the Left of which was on the Tagus, their Right on Casalegas, and their Front was hid by the river Alberche) during the night. I remained at the Convent until Genl. Hill's Division arrived, being ordered to Maj.-Genl. Tilson's for the day. Finding the French had retreated I crossed the river and proceeded through the French camp towards Casalegas, and returned by the bridge of the Alberche to Talavera. The Spanish Army began a pursuit of the French, whilst our advance halted near Casalegas, and the rest of our army returned to the neighbourhood of the town."

TALAVERA DE LA REYNA, *July* 24, 1809.

MY DEAR FATHER,

Since my last letter which was from Plasencia, the army has moved to this place; on the 17th inst. we marched from Plasencia; on the 22nd our advance fell in with that of the French at Gamonal, a town 2 leagues from this; they were driven out of that town and also from this; their main body continued posted on the other side of the Alberche a river which runs into the Tagus about 4 miles from this place. The next morning our troops moved towards the river intending to cross it by a ford near the right of the French, whilst the Spanish Army under General Cuesta was to cross it over a bridge on the left of the enemy. Sir Arthur however thought it prudent to put off the attack until the next morning, particularly (it is said) by desire of General Cuesta; accordingly our army as well as that of the Spaniards was put in motion this morning about 2 o'clock with the intention of forcing the passage of the river at daybreak; this would I daresay have cost us a great number of men, and I much doubt if the Spaniards would have been able to force the bridge as the enemy has had so much time to prepare us a warm reception. Upon reaching the bank of the river we were not a little surprised to find that they had all left their position the day before, and their camp on the other side deserted; we found that they had retreated during the night or early this morning. Our troops are ordered to halt here till to-morrow, which appears to be a good arrangement, as we should only fatigue our troops by an useless pursuit. The Spanish Army are in full march after them: they are very numerous but we do not think they will fight well, but it is impossible to say; they certainly ought to behave well in this country. The French Army are calculated at 18 or 20,000 men; they have another under Sebastian near Toledo of about 17,000 men; it is thought therefore that they mean to unite their force before they give us battle.

During the march from Plasencia to this town I was again sent forward to reconnoitre; I went up the river Teitar and along the right flank of the French to Arenas; I went with a column of Portuguese and Spaniards under Sir. R. Wilson who as usual behaved extremely kind to me. From Arenas I (with my servant only) crossed the French patrols and videts and rejoined the British Army at Oropesa; there I found Sir Arthur and informed him that Sir R. Wilson was on the right of the enemy; Sir Arthur then desired me to return to Sir Robt. Wilson that night and gave me an escort of Spanish dragoons with which I found Sir R. and returned to the army at Gamonal. I have had several providential escapes of being taken prisoner—was obliged to go across the country, avoiding the roads, etc. I am greatly indebted to the peasants of the country who always informed me when the enemy's patrols were near, as well as the best way of avoiding them.

Our promotion is come out and I am now living with Colonel Fletcher as his Adjutant which I hope I shall continue to do for some time. I am extremely well in health and spirits and hope you all continue so. . .

R. Jones.

Tuesday passed off in quiet; two of the Engineer officers being ordered to reconnoitre the Tagus and the Alberche, respectively.

Wednesday, July 26, also passed off quietly:—" Rode this day to Casalegas and ordered the entrenching tools from the German Brigade to the Guards. The Spaniards returned to the bridge over the Alberche this evening, the French having turned upon them. The town began to be crowded with the Spanish fugitives."

Thursday, July 27. " At daybreak rode along our camp to find the entrenching tools under charge of Corpl. Black; at last I discovered him near the entrance of the town. I then followed Colonel Fletcher who had gone with Sir Arthur to see General Cuesta at the bridge of the Alberche; on the way I overtook Foster; after waiting a short time on the other side of the river they all returned, as did Foster and myself. As soon as we were all in the town, the Col. informed us that at 11 o'clock we were to begin constructing a Redoubt for ten guns which is to be on rising ground forming the centre of the position to be occupied by the British and Spanish troops in the event of an attack being made by the enemy. We immediately began to lay it out, and a party of 200 men from Colonel ——'s Brigade were set to work; this party was relieved at 3 o'clock by one of the same strength from Brigadier-Genl. Campbell's, soon after which the firing, which we had heard for some time towards Casalegas, became nearer and our troops began to take up their ground in the position. At 6 o'clock this line was completed and ready, whilst a cannonade continued advancing rapidly towards our centre from the Convent near the Alberche. At 7 o'clock the enemy were close to our line, and the working-party took to their arms; another party at this moment arrived to relieve the former, but were, by Sir Arthur ordered to return to their regiments. The Spaniards whose left were in the redoubt at the same time commenced a brisk fire, but without anything opposed to them at which it could be directed. After waiting to collect the tools which were scattered about, I joined Col. Fletcher, and we proceeded towards our left where a heavy and running fire had just commenced; this soon after

35

ceased and we found Maj.-Genl. Hill's Division in quiet possession of the little hill which formed our left. The remainder of the night we rode amongst our line, but were not able to find Sir Arthur; at length we lay down under a tree to sleep, but were roused in a quarter of an hour by firing again which continued at intervals until daylight.

Friday, 28th July. At dawn this morning Col. Fletcher and myself found Sir Arthur on the hill which formed the left of our position, and the enemy's line (having several batteries along their front) drawn up opposite our left and centre. About 5 o'clock a heavy cannonade commenced by signal from the enemy and which was soon answered by our artillery; this was immediately succeeded by an attack upon the high ground upon our left and which was obstinately contested. During this time I was ordered by Col. Bathurst to find the cavalry and direct them to proceed up a valley which lay between the small hill we had occupied and a range of rocky heights. I first met the Duke D'Albuquerque to whom I communicated this order, and shortly after saw Genl. Fane moving up with the Heavy Dragoons; after this I returned to Sir Arthur through a heavy fire and found the enemy had been repulsed. The cannonade continued until the middle of the day when a short lull took place whilst the enemy might easily be seen cooking at a distance in the rear. Soon after, a general attack upon our whole line commenced; this was first repulsed by Brigadier-Genl. A. Campbell's Brigade on the right, and 19 cannon and some standards, etc., taken was the result of his charges. At the same time the centre under Lt.-Genl. Sherbrooke came to the bayonet and drove the enemy a considerable distance, but were obliged to retire rather precipitately, their left flank being totally exposed to the fire of the French Batteries which at that time nearly enfiladed the whole of our centre line; this was ably supported by the 1st Battalion, 48th Regiment, which had been ordered by Sir Arthur to cover their retreat, and which Regiment formed and kept possession of our ground until the guards rallied, when, coming once more to the charge, the French retired in every direction. During this time the enemy repeated their attempt on the hill on our left by moving three heavy columns along the valley to the north; this movement was rendered useless by the very gallant charge of the 23rd Light Dragoons which Regiment suffered extremely, but the enemy were prevented deploying from the close column they had formed in, the remainder of the day. The Heavy Dragoons continued in line directly in front of these columns and effectually kept them in check. After having thus defeated this general attack we remained tolerably quiet until dark, when the Col. and myself dismounted in a vineyard, between the bivouac of Sir Arthur and our line. We were fortunate enough to procure a little biscuit and wine from the Commissary who had brought a little for headquarters and had a good night's sleep.

Saturday, July 29th. At daybreak this morning the Col. and myself were upon the hill on our left, and waited anxiously for sunrise to ascertain where the enemy were; in a short time we had the pleasure of seeing they had all quitted the field during the night, and had thus given us complete possession of the Field of Battle. We immediately rode to Sir Arthur, and Col. Fletcher communicated this information to him, at which he seemed pleased, and sent us into Talavera to desire Capt. Canning, his A.D.C., to inform General Cuesta; after meeting him we returned to the hill and from thence rode along our line to the town of Talavera; on our way we met Mulcaster who had just arrived from reconnoitring the Tagus. We found Goldfinch and Forster were both well, and that Stanway was slightly wounded in the belly. We went to the Col.'s Quarters at Talavera and found poor Boothby with his leg badly wounded ever since the night of the 27th July; I went directly for Fitzpatrick, Surgeon to the Ordnance, and luckily found him; he said that amputation was the only chance of saving his life, and very soon after he performed the operation about $2\frac{1}{2}$ in. above the knee; from that time Boothby gradually got better. I sent in a return of killed and wounded, and then went with Lt. Forster to sketch the Field of Battle.

July 30th. Rode with Forster the other side of the Tagus and sketched its course as well as that of the Alberche; the enemy's posts upon that river still. Next morning rode with Capt. Chapman over the Battle Field.

August 2nd, the army ordered to march to-morrow morning; great uncertainty which road we shall take.

TALAVERA, *July* 29, 1809.

My DEAR FATHER,

Through divine mercy I have once more to let you know that I am very well in health and have been preserved unhurt in one of the most dreadful battles that has lately been fought; and our loss has been extremely great, as has been that of the enemy; the newspapers will give you the Gazette account of the affair. A private soldier of the 71st Regiment, in describing the earlier battles of the war, gives a vivid picture of the characteristic traits of the opposing troops:—" They (the French) came upon us crying and shouting, to the very points of our bayonets. Our awful silence and determined advance they could not stand; they put about and fled." And again;—" How different the duty of the French officers from ours! They, stimulating the men by their example; the men vociferating, each chaffing each until they appear in a fury. After the first huzza, the British officers restraining their men, still as death— ' Steady, lads, steady!' is all you hear, and that in an undertone." And on another occasion—" Down they came shouting, as usual; we kept them at bay, in spite of their cries and formidable looks. How different their appearance from ours! their hats set round with feathers, their beards long and black gave them a fierce look; their stature was superior to ours; most of us were young; we looked like boys; they like savages.

But we had the true spirit in us ; we foiled them in every attempt." The
French have now retired beyond the river Alberche to their old position,
but whether they mean to remain there, retreat, or attack us again, it is
impossible to say. Fortunately for us the Light Brigade have just arrived
and will make up for the numbers we lost yesterday. We are very much
in want of provisions, which I believe prevented our moving forward
some days ago. I would send you a longer letter, but it is with difficulty
I can get *this Note* taken by the officer who takes the Dispatches. Capt.
Boothby was wounded by a musquet ball in the calf of his leg and
has been obliged to suffer amputation. Lt. Stanway was struck by a
ball which spent itself in passing thro' his horse. . . . I was
with the Colonel near Sir Arthur during the whole time, and of course
had a great number of narrow escapes for which I desire to return thanks
to God. . . .

RICE JONES.

Indirect evidence of the privations of the army during these
operations is afforded by Lord Wellington's General Orders : thus,
under date, Talavera de-la-Reyna, August 2, 1809, he writes, "The
soldiers plunder the inhabitants bringing in provisions, notwithstanding
the repeated orders upon this subject, and the knowledge which they
all have, that this practice must tend to their own distress." And
again, on the 9th of August—"The soldiers themselves render the
difficulties of the moment greater than they would otherwise be by
their irregularity, as they seize and plunder the mules coming in with
provisions, by which the good and regular soldiers of the army are
deprived of their just share."

August 3rd. The army marched this morning from Talavera back
to Oropesa, in order to attack the force which was coming upon our
rear from Plascencia, under Marshal Soult. We were quartered in a
Nunnery. Whilst at dinner in the evening, Goldfinch informed us
that a Council of War was then sitting and that it was reported the
enemy were within a League of us and that probably we should be
attacked before daylight ; we made the necessary preparations and
then went to sleep.

August 4th. The army were out at daylight this morning ; soon
after, General Cuesta and the Spanish troops came pouring in upon us,
having quitted Talavera and deserted our sick ; it was soon understood
that we should be obliged to cross the Tagus at Puente del Arzobispo,
and accordingly our baggage and sick began moving there at daybreak. At half past 7 o'clock we marched from Oropesa, halted
at Puenta de Arzobispo and got something to eat ; we then slept in
a wood which our army occupied, about a mile from the bridge.

August 5th. At 7 o'clock the army marched and halted in
advance of this place (Paralidas) which was Hd. Qrs. Col.
Fletcher, Chapman and myself were billeted upon a small cottage ;
we were very short of provisions. Next morning the army marched
at 7 as usual, halted at Mesa del Ibor ; the Light Brigade advanced

towards Almaraz. *August 7th.* "Began our march as usual with Hd. Qrs. : very soon returned, procured a guide with whom we went to the Bridge of Almaraz where we found a Spanish post on this side of the Tagus and a French one on the opposite. The Col. fixed upon the sites of some batteries to defend the passage of the river ; during our operations we were a little disturbed by the fire of the enemy. From thence we went to Roman Gordo which was the quarters of the Light Brigade, and on to Deleytosa where we found Hd. Qrs. established. Next day Capt. Chapman was sent to the Bridge of Almaraz to construct the batteries."

August 11th. The army marched from Deleytosa ; Hd. Qrs. were fixed for the night at Jaraicejo,—"the town is entirely deserted and mostly in ruins." Next morning, "the Col. and myself pitched a marquee, it being impossible from the number of fleas, and the quantity of dirt to sleep in the village ; very much in want of provisions." *August 13th.* "Rode with the Col. to Las Casas del Puerto to see Genl. Craufurd who occupies that place and the neighbouring passes. From the Puente de Almaraz we had a fine view over the country between the Tagus and Teitar, and we thought we perceived the dust of a French Column north of the latter river.

August 15th. Accompanied the Col. to the town (Truxillo) ; the place being quite full of Spanish troops we with difficulty obtained admittance into a Quarters : we were obliged to remain in a cobbler's shop, where however we enjoyed the luxury of a good sleep upon *Matto*, and also some tolerable bread and wine for supper ;—N.B. The first wine we tasted from Talavera. *August 16th.* Searched the Castle and town of Truxillo, along with Col. Fletcher and a Priest, to find timber of a sufficient length to repair some of the bridges over the Tagus. Our search proved ineffectual ; I was therefore desired by the Col. to proceed to Caceres whilst he returned to Hd. Qrs. and reported the result of our search. Accordingly I left Truxillo with a Spanish Lt.-Col. who was acquainted with the resources of the town."

Our author remained three days at Caceres, which contained about 3,000 inhabitants, and had never been plundered by the French. His mission proving fruitless, he rejoined the army on August 20th :—
"Upon my arrival I met the Col. and Chapman endeavouring to make good their billet upon a house which, as well as the rest of the town (Truxillo) was full of Spanish officers ; in order to effect this we were obliged to have recourse to the Junta, etc., but at last succeeded in getting miserable accommodations." While here he visited the remains of the tomb of Pizarro, etc., "it has been defaced and the church nearly destroyed by the French."

"It was this gloomy city, situated on a black eminence," wrote W. Beckford, "that gave birth to the ruthless Pizarro, the scourge of the Peruvians, and the murderer of Atabaliba : the nakedest and most dreary region I ever beheld."

August 23. "Halted at Medellin, where grapes were obtained for the first time; in the evening I rode with the Col. over the field of battle between the French under Marshal Victor and the Spanish under Cuesta when the latter was completely routed. The enemy appear to have received the attack of the Spaniards in a perfect plain; their left being upon the river, and their right a little east of the town. We afterwards visited the fine old castle." Thence on to Merida on August 24th, where a halt was made till the end of the month;—"the army was hutted in the environs; the weather was intensely hot; the evenings we generally spent in riding about the neighbourhood which abounds in Roman antiquities, particularly the remains of an aqueduct, of Temples of Diana and Mars, and an Amphitheatre and a Triumphal Arch (still perfect)."

September 2nd. The army marched for Badajoz which was reached next day. "Here the Col., Chapman, and myself were billeted upon a Dignitary of the Church and remained idle for some time."

TRUXILLO, August 25, 1809.

MY DEAR FATHER,

My last letter was from Talavera the day after the Battle; in it I had only time to let you know of my welfare and since then no opportunity has occurred of writing to you. You are no doubt before this time in possession of full details of the glorious although fatal results of those days; and I have only to express my gratitude to God who so wonderfully preserved me during the dreadful slaughter that took place and was I believe never exceeded amongst so small a number of men. Our total number, according to returns that day did not exceed 20,000 men, whilst the enemy had, according to their own accounts 45,000, but it is generally thought they had more in the field. We lost about 5,000 altogether, and the French not less than 10 or 11,000. . . . From Jaraycejo, where we halted ten days, we moved yesterday to this town. For some days before the Battle of Talavera provisions became very scarce, and for some days we were all without anything except what accident threw in our way; we have never tasted wine or anything of that kind until we came here; the roads were very bad and the weather extremely warm. I am however very happy to find that we have at last begun to retreat in earnest. It is understood that we are to take a position for the present upon the frontiers of Portugal; we can at present do just as we please as I fancy the French have no idea of attacking us, and we cannot possibly attack them, our cavalry being completely done up, and nearly half our men either sick or wounded. Sickness is daily increasing, and I have little doubt we shall soon see England. No good I am convinced can ever be done for these people. . . .

RICE JONES.

CHAPTER FOUR

THE English troops—Napier tells us—were now distributed in Badajoz, Elvas, Campo Mayor and other places, and this eventful campaign of two months terminated.

On the whole, it has been unfortunate, though relieved by the victory of Talavera. The general loss of the British—Napier goes on to state—was considerable. Above 3,500 men had been killed, or had died of sickness, or fallen into the enemy's hands. 1,500 horses had perished from want, exclusive of those lost in battle; the soldiers were depressed, and a heart-burning hatred of the Spaniards was engendered by the treatment all had endured. To fill the cup of disaster the pestilent fever of the Guadiana, assailing bodies which fatigue and bad nourishment had already predisposed to disease, made frightful ravages; dysentery, that scourge of armies, raged, and in a short time several thousand men died in the hospitals.

The British General had learnt a lesson which was not forgotten during the rest of the war—that no reliance was to be placed on Spanish co-operation. At the same time, he was determined to protect the Spanish peasantry from the predatory excursions of his soldiers, as was made manifest to the whole army by his orders on the subject. Thus under date September 7th, 1809; " Notwithstanding the repeated orders given out upon the subject, the soldiers of the 4th Division of Infantry plundered beehives, in the neighbourhood of Badajoz : it is impossible these outrages can be committed daily, without the officers obtaining some knowledge of it. The officers with the army do not appear to be aware how much they suffer in the disgraceful and unmilitary practices of the soldiers, in marauding and plundering everything they lay their hands upon. The consequence is, the people of the country fly their habitations, no market is opened, and the officers, as well the soldiers, suffer in the privation of every comfort and every necessity, excepting their rations, from the neglect of the former, and the criminal misconduct of the latter." And again, September 12th ; " The 4th Division having again, in three instances plundered beehives, etc., etc.," severe punishment was meted out to the entire division, " till the soldiers shall have been discovered who have been guilty of these outrages."

During the pause that ensued, while the army was settling into quarters about Badajoz, some interesting occurrences are thus briefly alluded to by our diarist.

Sept. 9th. We this day received the Gazette account of the Battle of Talavera ; His Majesty's thanks in General Orders, and also letters from our friends in England.

Sept. 17th. Dined for the first time with Sir Arthur Wellesley ; after dinner we drank his health as Viscount Wellington, when he first assumed the title.

Oct. 7th. This day Lt.-General Sherbrooke was invested with the Order of the Bath for his services at Talavera.

BADAJOZ, *September 12th,* 1809.

MY DEAR FATHER,

. . . I have also received a letter from you in which you were kind enough to desire that I would draw upon you for what money I might want; I beg to return you many thanks for your continued and more than fatherly goodness and forethought on my account ; but am happy that I am able to go on without troubling you at this moment. From the nature of my duty as Adjutant, Qr.-Mr. and Paymaster to the R.M. Artificers, and indeed from the known good conduct of our officers, I can get whatever money I want from the Ordnance Paymaster, subject to a settlement at the end of our campaign ; should it soon close I fear I shall be a little in want when we arrive in England ; but if it continues a few months longer I trust I shall be pretty clear with the agents. This you can account for when you recollect the expense I have been at for horses, etc., and indeed although we endured for some time every priva-tion of meat, drink, etc., short of absolutely starving, yet even at that moment we spent a good deal of money from the avidity with which every morsel of anything eatable was bought up at any price. Since I have been Adjutant I have lived with Col. Fletcher, and indeed manage the table, etc. ; this is of course more expensive than living with another of our officers when attached to divisions, but at the same time it is more comfortable, as the Col. always gets a quarter near Sir Arthur's, and as the nights begin to get colder it is pleasanter sleeping in a house than in the field with the troops. It is now extremely warm in the day and rather cold in the night, which is very unhealthy and may perhaps account for the number of our sick, which is more than 10,000 including the wounded we left behind at Talavera. Our cavalry still continues in a very bad state. General Cattin Craufurd has this day joined us with seven or eight new regiments but for what purpose it is impossible to say ; we begin to suspect that Ministers are mad enough to think of continuing to support the allies we have found in this country ; if so I doubt not we shall do our duty in the next general battle, but should not be surprised if it ends in our ruin ; we cannot afford to gain another victory at the price we paid on the field of Talavera. Out of less than 18,000 men which was our total that morning, 5,300 were either killed, or wounded, or taken before the action ended, and we have been obliged to leave 2,200 and odd behind at Talavera who of course have fallen into the enemy's hands (by the bye we have heard from Boothby of ours who lost his leg ; the French Army are vying with each other who should show our wounded the greatest attention). At Plasencia we left 600 sick, at Oropesa 200, and they are daily dying in the hospital at Elvas. You will think this a gloomy account, but I assure you it is perfectly correct, and so far from being in the dismals or melancholy, whilst writing this, you must know that I am in high spirits, that the weather is fine, and that we all feel not a little proud and gratified at the very handsome manner in which the King has been pleased to notice our conduct and to acknowledge it in General Orders to the rest of the army. I really think we ought all to have medals as well as the officers commanding corps ; but at all events we expect to have Talavera on our appointments, etc.

I wrote to you last from Truxillo, since that we marched to Merida, and from thence, after halting 10 days, we arrived here on the 3rd instant. The army are all near this town. . . . Head Qrs. are here. This place is very strongly fortified for a Spanish town ; but its situation is rather unfortunate, being commanded on most sides ; it is about 120 miles from Lisbon to which city runs a good and level road. I suppose we shall halt here until the French choose to drive us from hence. This is a good large town and has never been plundered ; everything may be had, but unreasonably dear. . . .

I have some idea of drawing a plan of the Battle of Talavera upon thin bank paper as soon as I have time and sending it in a letter to him—(Sir W. W. Wynn) do you think he would like it ? You have not told me how Hollyhock goes on ; I begin to think I shall still want him before this year is ended. I wish much I could get a newspaper sent ; it is the greatest curiosity we can get ! If we are not likely to quit this country soon, I wish much to have a newspaper at least once a week ; I would write to Mr. Wharton about it, but I fear it would be very uncertain from him ; the person at Foreign Department of the Post Office is the best if you know them. I sometimes see *Bell's Messenger* of one of our officers ; therefore I do not wish that. Is it possible to get the Cambrian, Shrewsbury, or Chester papers to see the Welsh news also ?

Your loving son,
Rick Jones.

While at Badajoz, Rice Jones took the opportunity of inspecting the neighbouring fortress of Elvas, on the Portuguese side of the frontier, and Fort La Lippe—so called after that distinguished soldier, the Count La Lippe, who had been sent at the request of the Marquis of Pombal, in 1762, by the British Government, for the purpose of reorganizing the Portuguese Army and commanding it during the war with Spain. The fort bearing his name is the sole remaining memorial of his work in Portugal : he designed it, and superintended its construction.

Elvas, previous to the French invasion, must have been a pleasant town. Beckford, on his visit to it in 1787, found the ramparts " laid out and planted much in the style of our English gardens, and forming very delightful walks."

Badajoz—apart from its military importance, was not without interest; for it was there that the Italian traveller, Baretti, met his old friend, Dr. Merosio, whose English wife could boast of the most extraordinary adventures that probably ever befell a woman of gentle birth. She had been in the four quarters of the world, and could speak several languages, inclu ling that of the native Indians in the neighbourhood of Goa, where she had resided as a maid-of-honour to the unfortunate Marchioness Tavora who was beheaded at Lisbon in 1758. She had also been in Japan with her first husband, a Dutch physician, to whom she was married at Batavia. After her return to Europe, she had been taken in a Portuguese ship by a Salee pirate, and would probably have passed her whole remaining life in captivity had she not been an Englishwoman ; for, as such, she was redeemed along with the crew of an English vessel called the *Litchfield* which had been wrecked on the Barbary coast. After three years' captivity, she had been land:d at Gibraltar, whence she wrote to her husband that during her residence in Morocco she had become a great favourite with the Sultana, and that the presents her mistress had made to her at parting would more than suffice to enable them to pass the remainder of their days in comfort. " A narrative of her life," adds Baretti, " would make a fine book, and if I see her in Italy, I will spirit her up to it, and offer her my services towards the work."

On October 8th Lord Wellington, accompanied by Col. Fletcher and Col. Murray set off for Lisbon, where they were followed by our author and several of his brother officers, halting at various places on the way, with varying accommodation. Thus at Vendas Novas, " We were billeted upon an Estalagem (Inn) where we were tolerably comfortable ; we were obliged to sleep upon straw beds, but procured a very fair kind of dinner." Crossing the Tagus at Aldea Gallega, the party landed at Lisbon on the evening of October 12th— " went to my old landlord, No. 12, Rua Larga de San Roque, who invited me to take up my abode in his house again, which invitation I was induced to accept."

The following entries all have reference to those extensive defensive works for the protection of the capital, and—if the necessity arose—for covering the embarkation of the British Army, which became known as the "Lines of Torres Vedras," and which Lord Wellington decided on constructing, after consultation with his Chief Engineer, Col. Fletcher.

" The determination to commence these works," (the Lines of Torres Vedras) says Sir John Jones, " may be dated from the Battle of Talavera, when it became apparent to the Duke of Wellington that the contest would, in the next campaign, devolve on the small body of veteran British and newly-raised Portuguese troops under his command, and a defensive system of warfare ensue."

Oct. 14th. Rode to Fort St. Julian to sketch the ground intended to be occupied with a work. *Oct. 15th.* I was this day employed in drawing a plan of the ground I sketched yesterday. *Oct. 16th.* Colonel Fletcher accompanied Lord Wellington on an inspection of the country towards Sacavem and Castanheira. *Oct. 23rd.* Col. Fletcher accompanied Lord Wellington to Setubal. *Oct. 25th.* This being the 50th anniversary of our Gracious King's accession to the throne, we went to the Opera where a suitable ballet was performed. *Oct. 27th.* Lord Wellington left Lisbon to join the army at Badajoz. *Nov. 2nd.* The Col. and all the other officers (Royal Engineers) who have arrived from the army set out for Sobral, leaving myself and two others in Lisbon.

LISBON, *October 22nd,* 1809.

MY DEAR FATHER,

I have been for some time most anxiously expecting to hear from you; your last letter being more than two months old. . . . As I know you are extremely good, and particularly about writing, I begin to think some of your letters have miscarried. I hope to God nothing has happened to prevent your writing.

You will no doubt be surprised to find this letter dated from Lisbon until I inform you that Lord Viscount Wellington set out from Badajoz for this place on the 8th instant, accompanied by a few of his staff, the Qr.-Mr.-Genl. and our Chief in whose suite I have travelled thus far, together with Capt. Chapman. There are a number of reports on the subject of this visit. I know that his Lordship and the Col. have been riding all over the country for 30 miles round, and have nearly knocked up Col. Fletcher's stud; from which it is easy to conclude that the ground to be occupied for the defence of Lisbon is a material part of the Commander of the Forces' business at this place. I will also tell you what is an impenetrable secret at present even to our officers; viz., that *all* our Corps are ordered from the army to a place called Castanheira, about 30 miles higher up and on the same side of the Tagus as this city. The Col. talks of setting out for Castanheira to-morrow or the next day; I of course shall accompany him, and understand there are a great number of works in contemplation. These measures look too much like a determination on the part of Ministers to defend Portugal to the last extremity; that extremity will certainly arise as soon as the French are able to advance in any force, and we shall then very likely have just such a scramble to get off as the army at Corunna had last year. If we are obliged to fight another battle I do not doubt but the victory will be ours; but an army in the state of ours at this moment cannot afford to purchase victories at the rate we paid for that of Talavera. These are not more my sentiments than those of almost every officer in the army—not excepting the Second in command, the Staff or Chief Engineer.

The above is the state of politics here; we are looking most eagerly for yours in England. We daily hear of new ministries, partial changes, etc., but know not what to think will be the result. The Ambassador, Mr. Villiers, quits this country shortly, and Sir Rt. Wilson goes home on leave, I believe, in the same packet with this letter; he talks of returning in two months.

In my last letter I mentioned my intention of sending Sir W. W. Wynn a sketch of the scene of action at Talavera, and had actually begun upon it when I was suddenly ordered to this place, since which time I have been unable to do anything more towards its completion. . . . Since writing to you last, I continue in good health, although I feel rather weakened or debilitated, which can easily be accounted for from the very exceptional heat we always experienced in Spain during the days, and the comparatively great cold of the night, which latter circumstance we of course felt more in consequence of sleeping out without cover and being in want of meat and drink. I have however great reason to be thankful I continue so well as I do, the army being in general in an unhealthy state still. Our future operations are likely to be for some time in a good country with plenty of provisions, etc., and, I fancy, without being eaten up by the rest of our army. I shall now conclude, begging you will be so good as to give my best love to my dear mother and to my dear brothers and sisters. . . . Since my last letter I have had the pleasure of remembering three of them on their birthday. . . . You see I keep a correct Roster.

I am, my dear father,
Your loving son,
RICK JONES.

During the next few months, Jones was actively employed on the construction of the works at the western extremity of the Lines of Torres Vedras. The actual commencement of these celebrated defences took place on the following dates, respectively :—St. Julian, November 3rd ; Monte Agraça (the great redoubt in the centre of the position, overlooking Sobral), November 4th ; Torres Vedras, November 8th.

Reverting to the Diary :—*November* 29. Rode to Sobral, where I mustered and paid the artificers. Returned to Lisbon after looking at the works.

December 9th. My dear father's birthday, may he enjoy very many and happy returns of it. The army began to move from Badajoz to the north of the Tagus. Sold the horse I bought at Zaza la Mayor for 30 Dollars.

LISBON, 11th November, 1809.

MY DEAR FATHER,

I am quite at a loss to account for my not having received a letter from you yet, and the more so as I know you are very regular about writing. The last letter I received from you was dated the 17th August immediately upon the receipt of my letters from Talavera; since that time I have written to you from Truxillo, from Badajoz, and lastly from this place on the 22nd ult. Three Packets arrived here a day or two ago, having been due for some time ; they have brought letters to the beginning of this month ; I fancied I was certain of receiving a letter at least amongst the three Packets, and you may perhaps conceive my disappointment at finding none. I assure you I begin to feel quite uneasy, fearing that something or other has happened to prevent you writing. To hear from you is the only comfort I can enjoy in this country, and I am now very melancholy at times in consequence of my present deprivation of that pleasure.

Lord Wellington left us here on the 27th ult., to join the army at Badajoz, and has since that gone to Seville. Our troops occupy their old line from Merida to Badajoz, and a most unfortunate line it has been for us. In one of my last letters I told you how very unhealthy the army were, and I now understand that the sickness increases rather than diminishes, so that if we occupy our present ground long (which is notoriously un-healthy even for the natives) our army will soon be in an extremely bad state to take the Field. Officers in a state of severe illness arrive here daily from the army, and many have been obliged to go to England. All the officers of our Corps, who, as I before informed you were ordered from the army, are now distributed at Fort St. Julian, Torres Vedras, Sobral and Castanheira; at three former places works are now throwing up; at the latter we are making accurate plans of some positions. I am the only officer here except Hamilton who continues so lame since he was wounded at Oporto that he cannot walk about, even in the house, without difficulty. I have had a good deal to do here since the Colonel has been gone; all his correspondence necessarily passes through Lisbon, where the Depôts of all kinds, as well as the heads of departments, are; for this reason, principally, the Colonel left me here when he went away; although I believe he was fearful that my health would perhaps suffer by much exertion out of doors, and thought I could be useful here, which I trust the event has proved. I am a good deal better and stronger than when I first came here; I have not yet been ill, although I am in general far from well; I am taking Bark at present. The Colonel behaves extremely kind to me in every respect. Although I volunteered accompanying him as usual, he would not allow me, until the doctor says I am stronger.

I am not certain whether I told you in my last letter that I am in my old Quarters; my landlord very civilly kept them for my return, and insisted upon my occupying them, without another billet. I am billeted on the same house as the Colonel, which is usually the case; but, however, as our accommodations were not on the grandest scale, I determined to comply with my landlord's kind wishes. With assurances of my best love to my dear mother, and to all my dear brothers and sisters,

I remain, your affectionate son,

RICE JONES.

P.S.—Be so good as to make my compliments, etc., which I generally trouble you with, to Sir W. W. Jones and all the family. Let me know what is going on in England and also in Wales. We cannot imagine what will become of us amidst all the changes, etc., which are taking place.

LISBON, December 16th, 1809.

MY DEAR FATHER,

It was with great pleasure that I received your kind letter of the 20th ult. two days ago, and found you all still enjoyed your health; many thanks for the enquiries and directions you have sent me. I am now very well thank God, and feel as strong as ever. I had quite forgotten that Mr. Steed was in the Royal Dragoons; they are quartered at Belem, about 3 miles from this city. I will call upon Mr. Steed when I ride that way next, for I like much to see any of my own, or of my dear father's acquaintances; I recollect him very well when I was a Cadet. I am very much obliged for the news you give me; you cannot imagine how eager we all are to know what is going on in England; our fate will depend, I suppose, in great measure upon the stability of the Ministry. If you are in London, will you have the goodness to see if it is possible to send me a weekly newspaper; I understand the only way of ensuring its regular arrival is by getting it from the person who is at the Foreign Branch of the General Post Office. I sometimes see *Bell's Messenger*, but as it belongs to another of our officers, it very often happens that he is not quartered with us, and we then, of course, miss it. I believe there is one weekly paper (I think the *Phœnix*) which has the Gazette Promotions in it, but of this I am not certain. You will very likely think that the Promotions will not much concern me; but I must remind you that I do not expect to be many months of my present rank in the Service. As I form part of the Colonel's family, he will, I know, be glad of my getting a paper, for he has only Motley's Portsmouth one, which arrives but seldom, and then about a month or two in arrears.

Col. Fletcher has been here about nearly a fortnight, but is now gone again upon his circuit of the Works in this vicinity; he has determined upon my remaining here as the most central spot to conduct his correspondence. Everything in our Department goes on as well as can be wished in this country; but it is said that such was not the case with the Army before Flushing. Pray tell what is said about it in England; we of course wish to know how the Corps get on in other parts of the world; but are very seldom favoured with intelligence. Capt. Goldfinch remains here to superintend and report upon the works the Portuguese have been throwing up near here. Ross is gone back to join the army; he begged his compliments to you and my dear mother. The Colonel talked, whilst he was here last, of endeavouring to obtain Lord Wellington's permission to join the army when he next returned to Lisbon, as by that time (about three weeks or a month) the Works will be so far completed as not to require his presence. If he goes, I shall of course go with him, for he has repeatedly promised me that if he is in action I shall be so likewise. The others, I fancy, will remain until everything is completed. The Colonel has some anxiety to join the army, thinking it probable the French may receive the reinforcements which will undoubtedly be sent them, sooner or later, to enable them to attack us before April or May. Be that as it may, I am glad our army has quitted Spain—I hope for ever; it has been an unfortunate country for British armies. On your Birthday (which I assure you did not pass without many a sincere wish that you may enjoy many, very many happy ones yet) the army began their march towards Portalegre, and are to cross the Tagus at Villa Velha and Abrantes; the latter place is to be once more Head Quarters; our advance will be at Castello Branco; Abrantes being only 90 miles off, with a good road, plentiful country, and some good positions for defence, and the river Tagus navigable all the way up, is in every way a preferable

situation to the banks of the unhealthy Guadiana, from Merida to Badajoz.
I do not doubt but our troops will soon be restored on the banks of the
Tagus to that health which they almost all lost on the banks of the
Guadiana. I am as unfortunate as ever in horses; a beast of a baggage-
horse that I bought whilst on a reconnoitring expedition in Spain, was
upon my arrival here completely knocked up, as well as myself. Ever
since I have been endeavouring to recover him for a march, but to no
purpose. I was therefore glad to accept 30 dollars for him yesterday, as
he was daily getting worse. I gave 60 dollars for him; you will therefore
perceive my loss is 30. I expect I shall be obliged to give about 80 dollars
to replace him. My servant William behaves extremely well; he has
been very ill indeed, but is now tolerably well recovered. . . .

Your very affectionate son,
RICE JONES.

P.S.—I now learn that part at least of our army are to march through
Leyria, and very probably thro' Coimbra; this is to me utterly inexplic-
able; however, a few days must inform us when and wherefore these
movements are made.

December 17th. Taken ill this evening. *December 22nd.* The
first day I have been able to dine at the Mess since Sunday, having
been confined by a sore throat. *December 27th.* Rode to Torres
Vedras through Loisa to the left of the Cabeca de Monte Chico.
Mustered and settled with the artificers, and afterwards went round
the works. *December 29th.* Rode from Torres Vedras to Sobral,
thro' Runa, Ribaldeira, and Dous Portas; settled with the artificers.
December 30th. Rode from Sobral to Aruda, from thence to Castanheira. *Sunday, December 31st.* Went to Carrigada with Chapman;
fixed upon the Quinta of the Conde de Loisa for our quarters. Rode
to Lisbon to dinner.

And here a few words of explanation with respect to the manner in
which the works were constructed may prove of interest to the non-
professional reader. Major-General Sir John T. Jones, R.E., who, as
a captain was employed on the Lines, tells us that the position and
nature of the several works having been determined on, these were
pressed forward ; and that the young officers of Engineers, now, for
the first time, placed in charge of extensive districts "exerted themselves with a zeal which knew no limits, and everywhere throughout
the Lines a spirit of honourable emulation proved highly advantageous
to the progress of the work." The peasantry of the country were put
into requisition as labourers ; overseers, directors, and artificers were
furnished by a detachment of British infantry, and " no petty cavils
about official forms of expenditure were allowed to impede the supply
of materials and stores."

It was a novel *rôle* for young officers, and the duties proved
excessively arduous ; but there were compensations. To quote from
Sir John Jones :—" The British officers, spread singly over a space of

150 square miles of country, and billeting themselves in the best and most convenient houses, were everywhere treated with civility and kindness by the inhabitants, and a general readiness was shown by the upper classes to admit them to the familiar society of their families, which led to many sincere and disinterested friendships being contracted between the individuals of the two nations. Indeed it is but a tribute of justice to the Portuguese gentlemen and peasantry of Estramadura to state that, during many months of constant personal intercourse, both public and private, the latter ever showed themselves respectful, industrious, docile and obedient ; whilst the former in every public transaction evinced much intelligence, good sense, and probity, and appeared in their domestic relations kind, liberal, and indulgent, both as masters and parents."

In order to realize the anomalous nature of the situation created, we must try and picture what the attitude of our own people would have been, *vis-à-vis* of a number of young Portuguese officers placed in charge of the defensive works which were being constructed along the south coast of England at the time of Napoleon's threatened invasion. The truly admirable behaviour of the Portuguese, of all classes, under very trying circumstances was worthy of commendation.

CHAPTER FIVE

Sunday, Feb. 4th. Took up my old Qrs. in Lisbon. I find that the 79th and 94th Regts. have arrived here from England, under Genls. Picton and Hon. W. Stewart. Saw the 79th Regt. Inspected in the Rocio by Genl. Stewart.

Feb. 6th. In consequence of advices having been received from Cadiz of the French having pushed thro. the Sierra Morena, entered Seville and appeared before Cadiz, the 79th, 94th, and 87th Regts. began to embark this afternoon under command of the Hon. W. Stewart. Dined at the Artillery Mess ; but both Owen's and Hughes' Companies (just landed from England) receiving orders to embark whilst we were at dinner, every person was hurried and in a bustle this evening.

Feb. 7th. Capt. Goldfinch and myself purchased a Gold Snuff Box, for which a subscription was raised by the officers of the Corps in Portugal, and which is to be presented to the Landlord of our office in 33, Rua de Alecrim.

Feb. 9th. Lord Wellington, etc., went to Fort St. Julian ; the Col. and Capt. Goldfinch accompanied him.

Feb. 10th. The Col. set out with Lord Wellington upon his return to the army thro. Castanheira. I went to the Rua das Condes Theatre. It was on the occasion of this visit to Castanheira, that Lord Wellington—according to Sir John Jones—perceiving that it was a line open to be turned, ordered the works to be filled in. This explains the following entry in the Diary :—" Found Lt.-Col. Fletcher at Torres Vedras, and heard of the demolition of our works at Castanheira, (Feb. 13th)."

Feb. 15th. Procured Qrs. for the Col. and myself at Eiriceira where I am to remain in charge of the works in that neighbourhood.

Feb. 16. Making out my Reports upon the roads I have lately reconnoitred, and copying part of Lt.-Col. Fletcher's Report upon Peniche.

Feb. 18th. Removed my Qrs. from Mafra to this place (Eiriceira).

Rice Jones remained here, in charge of the works under construction, until May 7th. A few extracts from the Diary will suffice to give an idea of his daily duties :—*Feb. 19.* Picked out the Redoubts near the 3 Mills above Carvoeira, in readiness for the 2 Companies of the

Militia of Figueira to begin to-morrow ; tasked the men in parties of 8 each ; they work extremely hard and willingly ; reduced the parties to 5 ; the ground at the Redoubts begins to be very hard and rocky ; Mr. Miller a Conductor of Stores arrived here, to relieve a Child of the name of A. *Feb.* 28. Met Capt. Chapman ; he fixed upon the spots to destroy the roads from Picanseira to Mafra ; pointed out the lines of the Redoubts to be begun ; and the several places where the roads leading to Marvao and Ribar Mar are to be destroyed ; the principal roads are to be prepared by means of mines ; all the others are to be broken up immediately.

Accommodation had to be provided for parties of Miners from the various British Regts. employed in breaking up the roads ; and parties of Peasants had to be set to work on the Redoubts ; all of which kept our author very fully employed. Then, from time to time, difficulties arose :—" Went to the Redoubts at Picanceira, found some of the Ericeira Peasants, but could not employ them, as they had brought no tools ; the day being very wet and stormy I was obliged to order all the working parties in ; there will be no work to-morrow, being a holiday."

March 8. Col. Fletcher arrived, and proceeded to inspect the spots fixed upon for destroying the roads ; he made some alterations. An experiment is to be made upon one of the mines which is intended to complete the destruction of the roads upon the advance of the enemy. We all returned to Ericeira for dinner ; the Col. and C. slept at the Qrs. I had prepared for them at the house of the Conceilleiro. Next day, Col. Fletcher visited various points of the coast, etc., and marked out spots for Redoubts ;—" it was a very wet and windy day."

Sunday, March 11. Rode with Capt. Ross to Mafra, and then went to Cintra by the paved road ; left our horses at the English Inn and walked to the Penha Convent ; just reached the top before the sun set. Went to the Capitao Mor, and settled with him that the Company of Ordonnances of San Joao de Lampadao shall assemble at Carvoeira on Wednesday.

March 24. Major Fras. Rapozo of the Portuguese Engineers arrived at Ereceira to take over part of the works ; Rice Jones paid a visit to a Quinta at Santo Isidoro where he intended occasionally, to take up his Qrs. and ordered a bed to be prepared ; and received intelligence of the arrival of several Engineer officers from England. Such an entry as the following is of frequent occurrence—" Paid the Companies of San Joao, etc., for the past week." *Apropos,* we learn from Sir John Jones that, the difficulty of supplying so many with food was met by the Engineer officers turning Commissary, and issuing rations of bread instead of an equivalent in wages.

April 16. Began fascining the Redoubts at Picanceira. (The

Fascine manufactory was in a wood near Fonte Boa dos Nabos and the greater part of the timber required for the gun platforms, magazines, etc., in the Redoubts was supplied from the Royal Park at Mafra).

April 17.   Met Col. Fletcher near Mafra, and after loading and preparing a Mine on the road below Ribar Mar ; viz.—Length of Box for Powder 15 ft. 10 in., 3¾ in. square inside ; Depth of mine 7 ft. ; Breadth of Road from 8 to 10 ft. at top, 12 ft. below ; we fired it ; the effect produced was only that of the blowing away the soil with which the Mine was loaded, to a short distance, and loosening the rock to about the level of the Powder ; but the cavity formed was nearly filled up by the earth which fell in upon the explosion taking place.

April 22.   Our diarist rode from Ereceira to Lisbon, passing a village (name illegible) " beautifully situated on the banks of a small rivulet, to the more beautiful scenes near Bellas, and from thence by Bemfica to Lisbon.   Went to my old Qrs. and found all as usual, well."

April 26.   " Capt. J. T. Jones ordered to relieve me at Ereceira ; I am directed to take up my abode at No. 33, Rua do Alecrim as soon as I have given up my District."   (The Capt. Jones mentioned above is better known as Major-General Sir John T. Jones, Bart., R.E., the Historian of the war, and of " Journals of the Sieges in Spain.")

Setting off again, on April 30, our diarist rode with the Col. to the marshes near Alhandra ; from thence, alone, to Aruda ; thence to the works at Monte Agraca (where, later on, he was destined to pass many weary and anxious hours, waiting for an enemy that would not attack) ; thence on to Sobral, just under the Great Work, and onwards, to Enaxara.   " Between Sobral and Enaxara," he writes, " near the village of Guisandeira the scenery is most romantically picturesque." With which statement I am in hearty accord ; in fact, I may say, from a personal investigation of this beautiful tract of country, that a tour of the famous Lines of Torres Vedras, will prove a revelation to most people, not only in respect of the enormous strength of the position selected by Lord Wellington for stemming the flood of invasion, but for the beauty of the scenery.

May 1.   " The day being very wet, Mulcaster and myself agreed to remain at home, which we did, and spent the day in reading and conversation very pleasantly."   The next few days were chiefly occupied in examining and making up Pay Lists, ready for handing over charge of the District.

May 7.   " Capt. J. T. Jones and myself rode along the works from Ribamar to Picanceira.   Gave up everything in the district to Capt. Jones, and sent my baggage and pony to Lisbon."   And on May 10. " Rode from Mafra through Bellas to Lisbon ; took up my Qrs. in this city."

His friend Capt. Goldfinch had the misfortune to lose his English mare, which died of a wound in the shoulder from an Ox-goad : and poor Capt. Hamilton who had been wounded at Oporto, died on May 20, and was buried in the new Factory Burying Ground ; the 2nd grave from the Hospital, on the South side of the centre walk, near a young Cyprus Tree.   *May 29.* " Took charge of our Mess at this place. Completed my 22nd year ; went to the Rua dos Condes (Theatre) in the evening."

June 1.   " Went with Mudge on board the *Marlborough* Packet* to procure for him a passage to England in her."

The following entry of same date calls for explanation :—" Bought 11 telescopes for the Signal Stations."   Rapid means of communication along the Lines of Torres Vedras being essential, signal stations, five in number were established on the most conspicuous positions ; the principal one, near the centre, being on the lofty mountain of Socorro, just above the village of Pero Negro, where Lord Wellington subsequently fixed his quarters.   The apparatus consisted of a mast and yard from which balls were suspended ; and there being no trained signallers available amongst the troops, Lord Wellington applied for and obtained the services of a party of seamen under their own officers, from the fleet in the Tagus.   And so expert did these men become after a little practice, that signals were passed from one end of the line to the other with undeviating accuracy, in seven minutes. It was for the signal-parties that the telescopes above-mentioned were purchased.†

June 4.   Goldfinch and myself rode to the Rocio, where the Regts. fired 3 volleys in honour of His Majesty's Birthday, and then marched past General Leith.

June 5.   Walked to the Royal Silk Factory with Mrs. Dalebarra and 2 other ladies.   The Royal Silk Factory, here mentioned, had a curious history.   It must be explained that, in consequence of the expulsion of the Jews from Portugal, by King Emanuel, in 1496, the decay of industry and manufactures commenced ; for the Jews, here,

---

* The *Duke of Marlborough*, commanded by Capt. John Bull, was one of the most famous vessels of the Post Office Packet Service.   While in her, that well-known officer fought more actions than any other Packet Officer. She was attacked on two occasions, while homeward bound from Lisbon, during the year 1810.   (The Post Office Packet Service, by A. H. Norway).

† (The following report from Capt. J. T. Jones to Col. Fletcher is of interest :—*July* 18, 1810. I am sorry I cannot give you a favourable account of the Signal Stations; the sailors say that the distance between the stations is too great, and that the masts are all too light for the yards ; on Sunday evening two were sprung ; they also complain of the telescopes. I have ordered stronger masts and yards to be prepared for each post, and if better telescopes can be procured in Lisbon, I shall not hesitate to authorize the purchase of them).

as in Spain, were the commercial backbone of the kingdom ; and although a few found their way back to Portugal and re-established industries, the fanatical outburst of Inquisitorial persecutions under John Vth caused a fresh exodus. Very curious too, were some of the methods resorted to by Ecclesiastics for repairing the ruin they had brought on the kingdom. Thus, a "dignified churchman," Southey tells us, founded a silk factory at Sobral, an ill-chosen situation, being a day's journey from Lisbon. But—alas ! 'tis not in mortals to command success ; the attempt failed, and the costly buildings were in ruins, when Southey was there.

Then the great Minister Pombal—whose hatred of the Jesuits led to their expulsion—tried his hand at the re-establishment of manufactures, and with a view to encouraging the silk industry, he imported nearly 20,000 mulberry plants from France, in 1771, and an equal number the following year, with the result that the produce of the Royal silk factory he had established at Lisbon, rose in one year, from 16,000 lbs. to 44,000 lbs. Another silk factory was established by the same Minister in an empty College of the Jesuits at Evora, " which, for want of support, soon fell to the ground," as happened to most of his manufactures," we are told by a well-informed writer.

With respect to the Royal silk factory at Lisbon, which, by the way, was protected by a severe prohibition of any importation of that article from abroad, some curious facts have come to light. Thus, even during Pombal's administration, it happened often that the looms were stopped merely through the want of money to keep them going, insomuch that the great warehouse of the factory was often without goods to meet the public demand, and the Minister was under the necessity of ordering privately, and in contravention to his own laws, silks to be smuggled from the French ships in the river, in the nighttime, and afterwards sold to the public as the produce of his own manufactory.

It is interesting, in view of the above facts, to find the Lisbon silk factory bravely struggling against fate—to say nothing of the handicap of a long and exhausting war—some thirty years after the fall of the great Minister who brought it into being.

What with frequent visits to Theatre and Opera, a constant succession of friends to dinner, and dining out at other Messes, our Diarist seems to have had a gay time in Lisbon. On June 21st, several brother officers came into Lisbon to see the Procession in honour of the Festival of Corpo de Deos, which was celebrated with all its wonted splendour —the war notwithstanding :—" The Rocio was very splendidly fitted up with Tapestry and Red Velvet Hangings, and the concourse of spectators very great."

Rice Jones' pleasant sojourn at Lisbon was about to be cut short— " The Col. having received permission to join the army, which he talks of doing shortly,"—accompanied, of course, by his Adjutant. Great events were impending on the North-Eastern frontier of Portugal, where Massena was massing his hosts for the third invasion of that unfortunate Kingdom. Ciudad Rodrigo was being besieged ; General Crawfurd and the Light Division were watching events on the Coa, and Lord Wellington had established his headquarters at Celorico. Under these circumstances—and in view of the work on the Lines being well advanced—it was natural that Lt.-Col. Fletcher, as Chief Engineer, should desire to be at the front.

The Diary contains the following abstract with respect to the work on which the writer had been employed for so many months :—

July 1.   Mem. of Works constructed.

	Works.	Men.
First Line	32	10,040
Second Line	65	14,600
San Julian	11	3,850

While, amongst his Papers are sundry Abstracts and Pay-Lists containing accounts of the daily expenditure, and number of men employed under his immediate superintendence.

It may be of interest to explain here how these defences, covering a vast extent of country, came by the designation they bear. A reference to the dates previously given will show that, except at the Monte Agraça, a point quite out of the beaten track, and almost unknown at that time to the British, the works at Torres Vedras were commenced three months before any other part of the Lines,— " which accidental circumstance," says Sir John Jones, " added to the previous celebrity of the Pass, caused their name to be given to the whole system of defence."

Note.—Copy.

Comdg. Rl. Engrs. Orders,
Mafra, 6th July, 1820.

As Lieut.-Colonel Fletcher, Captains Chapman, Squire, and Goldfinch are about to join the army, Capt. Jones will be left in the immediate command and superintendence of all works and other duties connected with the Engineer Department in this part of Portugal, and he is therefore to be obeyed accordingly.

(Signed)   R_D. Fletcher,
Lt.-Col. Comdg. Ryl. Engineers.

Copied from the original in Lieut.-Colonel Fletcher's handwriting— Rice Jones.

Quitting Lisbon on July 5th, Colonel Fletcher and party marched *via* Mafra, Torres Vedras, Peniche, to Alcobaca, where the party was—" most hospitably received by the good monks of that Convent ; we were supplied with a plentiful dinner ; and afterwards retired to good beds. Next morning, after breakfasting at the Convent, we went through the Chapel, Refectory and magnificent Kitchen belonging to it ; we then set out, and after viewing the church at Batalha and taking some refreshment at the Convent arrived at Leyria ; Col. Fletcher procured good Quarters at the House of Donna Maria do Candide, near the Bishop's Palace ; I slept at a tolerably good yellow house at the foot of the hill."

Little did the inhabitants of these beautiful spots divine the impending storm—already gathering on the frontier,—which, in a brief while, was destined to overwhelm them ; leaving nothing but ruin and desolation in its train.

Thence, the party proceeded through Pombal, Condexa—near which one of the Colonel's horses got entangled in a deep ditch, and was only extricated, with the assistance of the villagers—to Ponte de Murcella, where—writes the Diarist ;—" My quarters were in a little cottage most beautifully situated above the romantic little river Alva, from the old stone bridge over which this poor village takes its name." Very full details are given of the nature of the country traversed,—size and description of the villages, and exact distance between each, with remarks on the condition of the roads, bridges, etc. ; interesting only to anyone planning a tour through this part of Portugal.

The next halting place was San Jago, where quarters were only obtained through the kindness of Mr. Deputy Commissary-General Rawlings taking the party into his Quinta, where they all slept in one room. Next day, July 13th, they reached Celorico, with its narrow, dirty streets, where, again, quarters could only be got by the exertions of a friend. The town was occupied by Sir Brent Spencer and the 3rd Guards ; several other Regts. being quartered in the neighbouring villages. On arrival here, they first " heard of the skirmish on the 10th and of the death of Col. Talbot of the 14th Lt. Dragoons in it ; also, the account of the capture of Ciudad Rodrigo by the French was confirmed."

Meanwhile Lord Wellington had transferred his quarters to Alverca ; and being unable, for lack of troops, to save Ciudad Rodrigo, had made the best preparations he could to meet the impending invasion. For Massena, at the head of an overwhelming force of veteran soldiers was about to cross the frontier ; and it was clearly perceived that the only hope of saving Portugal was by assembling the numerically inferior and heterogeneous forces composing the allied army in the citadel which had been secretly constructed across the Lisbon Peninsula. It was at this crisis, says Sir John Jones, that rumours of an immediate invasion having reached Lisbon, a great impetus was imparted to the work going forward on the Lines. The intelligence had the further effect of stirring up the Portuguese authorities, on whose assistance and goodwill the execution of the design was in some measure dependent. The conscription for labour was now extended to a distance of more than 50 miles round, and at one period, although the middle of harvest, the workers on the Lines were augmented to more than 7,000. Even women and boys took their share, being paid respectively at the rate of one-half and one-fourth the price of men ;—though to be sure, anyone who has seen Portuguese women labouring in the fields would be inclined to rate their work at a much higher figure.

July 14th. Alverca. "Here we have once more been fortunate enough to rejoin the Head Qrs. of the army ; the Col. and Chapman dined with Lord Wellington. After some trouble I got quarters in the cottage of a Cobbler on the road to Guarda."

July 15th. From Alverca the Col., Chapman and myself set out early this morning, and upon our arrival at Almeida we called upon Brig.-Genl. Cox, the Governor, by whose permission we staid to dinner, and procured Qrs. for the night. After dinner we rode to Brig.-Genl. Crawfurd's Head Quarters at the village of Valdela Mula, about 4 miles from Almeida ; found Burgoyne there and went with him to Fort Conception. By the time we had walked round the Fort, and seen the mines prepared by Burgoyne for its destruction, the lateness of the evening made our quick return to Almeida desirable, to prevent our being shut out of that Fortress. Tormented all night by innumerable hosts of Bugs at my bad billet.

Describing the country traversed this day, the Diarist thus refers to the bridge over the Coa, which was destined to play such an important part in General Crawfurd's famous fight, a week later :—"Ascended a hill and then descended to the river Coa ; a stone bridge of 3 arches, forming 3 different lines, the bank steep and very rough ; ascended a long hill to Almeida ; the country perfectly open and flat to Valda Mula."

July 16th. While the Col. and General Cox were consulting upon the defence, etc., of Almeida, Chapman and I walked round the works. Breakfasted at the Governor's and met Major Napier of the 50th Regt. ; he went with a Flag of truce to Gallegos yesterday and saw General Loison there ; he says Lord Wellington will not fight a battle to relieve Almeida. General Crawfurd retired the Infantry of his Division at daylight this morning to Guinse, (?) leaving his cavalry to cover Fort Conception. We returned to Alverca.

July 17th. Col. Fletcher and myself dined at Head Qrs. Marshal Beresford dined there also.

Sir Augustus Frazer, who commanded the Royal Horse Artillery, thus describes a dinner with Lord Wellington :—"The party consisted of 28 ; Lord W. sits in the middle of one side. Fancy smiles at the eager looks which betray the anxiety to catch a smile from the hero of the day. A Count de Chaves and his boy were soon asleep; I and Col. Arentschild were ready to follow the example before we broke up; (at 11.30) heat, good cheer and champagne had made us all drowsy and stupid; all, however, seemed unnecessarily in fear of the great man; on his part he talked with apparent frankness."

July 21st. The French at daylight this morning drove in our outposts, and established themselves at Valda Mula. Burgoyne fired the mines at Fort Conception which answered perfectly; our videttes about 2 miles in front of Almeida this morning.

July 23rd. This evening and part of the night there was incessant and tremendous thunder and lightning with heavy rain.

July 24th. The rain continued violent the whole of this day, with thunder and lightning. Col. Fletcher and Chapman rode to Pinhel, and returned with the intelligence that the enemy, this morning, had driven the Light Division under General Crawfurd from before Almeida to the left bank of the Coa, with considerable loss. Napier, in his History, tells us that General Crawfurd " Had kept a weak division (4,000 British infantry, 1,100 cavalry and 6 guns) for three months within two hours march of 60,000 men ; but this exploit did not satisfy his feverish thirst for distinction, . . . he with headstrong ambition resolved, in defiance of reason and of the reiterated orders of his general, to fight on the right bank." And the historian, who was present as a captain in the 43rd, at this memorable but disastrous fight, describes the affair with all his wonted eloquence. In the sequel, Crawfurd brought his division over the Coa, but with a loss of 272 British, including 28 officers, and 44 Portuguese, killed and wounded. The French loss was over a thousand, but,— " with a conscription, and the nations of Europe to draw on, Massena could better have afforded twenty times that number than Wellington could afford the loss of his veterans of the Light Division."

July 25. The Light Division retired before daylight and took post near the village of Carvalhal; the German Legion bivouacked near this village (Alverca). Lord Wellington and Col. Fletcher rode towards the outposts at daylight; Chapman and I followed; hearing that everything was quiet, we returned. Next day, the Light Division retired to Freixeras 3 miles from here. *July 27.* The Col., Chapman and I rode out early; at Freixeras found the Light Division, also Ross, and his brother's troop of Horse Artillery; we continued our ride to the out pickets; finding everything quiet, returned to Head Qrs. Orders given to march to-morrow. Burgoyne and Thomson sent to mine the Ponte de Murcella.

July 28. At daylight the army retired from their ground near Alverca. The Light Division came into this town (Celorico), as did

Head Qrs. We find this town nearly deserted ; quartered in a white house, uninhabited and full of fleas.

Celorico, July 30. Col. Fletcher and myself rode in the evening along the banks of the Mondego, met a dragoon who informed us that Col. Wyndham, Comdg. the Ryl. Dragoons, had just been taken.

During the next few days,—"everything remained quiet, *in statu quo.*" But our Diarist had a sad misfortune—" My Batman having lost my Ass, deserted the night before last, or early yesterday morning,"—"the Col. and I took a ride with Ross, his brother, etc., to Val de Serra, a beautiful village about 2 miles south."

August 8. Went to Guarda, dined at General Coles'. The enemy have not broke ground before Almeida. Don Julian with a few of his troop pass through Guarda to Celorico. Massena said to be at Fort Conception with two Corps of his army. Deserters say they are preparing gabions, etc., for the siege of Almeida. The Portuguese peasantry on the frontier begin to show some enterprise. General Hill is still at Sarzidas ; he, it is supposed intends fighting on the Abita. On the other side of the beautiful Valley of the Mondego is the romantic village of Porco, the Head Qrs. of General A. Campbell's Brigade ; there are a number of large Quintas in this valley ; from here the road ascends by innumerable turnings up the heights to Guarda, an ancient city, the walls of which are old and incomplete on part of one side.* The Colonel sent to Mulcaster (at Guarda) to establish a Mast and Flag for a Telegraph to communicate with one to be erected at Celorico.

Next day, the Col. went to Guarda about erecting a Telegraph there. The Staff-corps under Capt. Ross' directions continue the preparations for erecting a Telegraph at the Castle (at Celorico). Chapman received a letter from Lord Mulgrave offering him the situation of Under Secretary ; it was dated 5th of May (Recd. Aug. 10) but for some unaccountable accident has been so long delayed.

Celorico, August 10. Lord Wellington publishes two letters from officers of the Army to a merchant at Oporto which had created considerable alarm in that city ; His Lordship requests that officers will be more careful in their future correspondence.

This brief entry—without comment, is thus alluded by Napier :— " an officer of the Guards, writing to a friend at Oporto, indiscreetly declared that Massena was advancing in front with a hundred thousand men, and eighty thousand more were moving in rear of the allies upon Lisbon. This letter was made public, and created such a panic amongst the English merchants in Oporto that one and all applied for ships to carry their families and property away." The senior Naval

---

* Built in 1197 as a defence against the Moors, at an altitude of 4,500 ft.

officer on the spot applied to Lord Wellington for instructions ; and his lordship, " to dry up this spring of mischief announced in general orders that he would not even seek for the authors of that and similar letters, being assured their sense and feeling would prevent a continuance of such pernicious correspondence."

The fact is that, ever since the Battle of Talavera a feeling of despondency with respect to the war in the Peninsula had been growing in England ; and when, in March, Ministers of the Crown asked for a sum of money for the defence of Portugal, it was opposed by a powerful and influential party, on the grounds of the utter hopelessness—as they declared, of continuing the struggle. Whi'e in the House of Lords, Lord Grenville speaking in the same lofty strain, declared that " it was a sacred duty imposed upon them to see that not one more life was wasted, not one more drop of blood shed unprofitably, where no thinking man could say that, by any human possibility such dreadful sacrifices could be made with any prospect of success." In short, " he would consider it nothing but infatuation to think of defending Portugal with such a force."

Despondency was by no means, however, confined to a party in England : It had infected Wellington's army in the field. Even Napier admits that " many British officers laughed at the notion of remaining in Portugal ; the major part supposed the campaign on the frontier to be only a decent cloak to cover the shame of an embarkation."

That these gloomy views were not shared by the army at large, however, is made clear by certain correspondence which has recently come to light :—" There is a very numerous body of officers in this army," wrote Capt. Dickson of the Artillery, (better known as Sir A. Dickson, who subsequently commanded the whole of the Artillery of the Peninsular Army under Lord Wellington), under date 27th of August, 1810, (the day of the fall of Almeida)—" who, either tired of the service, or having an idea the Portuguese won't fight, do nothing but put the worst colouring on the matter, dwelling on the impossibility of resistance against the immense force of the French, and the certainty of being obliged to embark in a short time ; and all this, without the smallest knowledge of disposition or locality beyond their own division or corps." While Capt. Warre, on Lord Beresford's Staff, writing two days later, to friends at home, was even more scathing in his remarks :—" I hate grumbling and croaking, and I think it most unsoldierlike in an army such as ours, even were we less strong. We must trust to the *fortune de la Guerre*, and the abilities of our generals. I wish that every English officer thought the same, and wrote less nonsense to their friends at home."

In truth, the position of the Commander-in-Chief at this critical juncture was no bed of roses ; the troubles and perplexities by which

Wellington was beset indeed would have broken the hearts of most men. For, in addition to the clamour of a formidable party at home, intent on throwing up the sponge and abasing the nation before the "man of destiny," as well as the disloyalty of certain officers in his own army, he had to face the unscrupulous hostility of the Portuguese Government, whose members, with scarce an exception, instead of exerting themselves in the national cause, not only opposed every measure necessary for the salvation of their country, but excited discontent amongst the populace. At length Wellington turned on these wretches, and with fierce rebuke warned them that " their miserable intrigues must cease, or he would advise his own Government to withdraw the British Army." But difficulties which would have driven weaker generals to the verge of despair, only steeled the nerves of this man of iron constitution and inflexible will.

CHAPTER SIX

To resume the Diary :—

August 12, 1810.   The Telegraph at the Castle completed.   Ross of the Artillery rode to Linhares, from whence he distinguished the signals made by the Portuguese Telegraph with one arm, fixed upon the Castle here (Celorico).   The French are reported to have retired from Penamacor towards Coria ; the peasantry have harassed them considerably during their stay in that neighbourhood.

August 13.   The Portuguese General Silveyra has taken a Battln. of the 3rd Swiss Regt. in the French service, in Puebla de Canabria, consisting of 400 men ; they had been shut up in that place from the 29th of July, previous to their surrender.

August 15.   The Telegraph at Guarda reports a skirmish to have taken place in front of the city, in which Capt. Cocks, 16th Lt. Dragoons, aided by the peasantry of the country had killed 4 and taken 18 of a party of the enemy.   Enemy said to be moving on our left.

August 18.   The army begins to get into motion towards the front, and reports of an immediate advance become prevalent. Mulcaster writes me from Guarda ;—" 17 *August*, 1810, 8 p.m.   The firing has been very brisk from Almeida during this day.   The enemy are certainly constructing a Battery on the Knoll opposite the face of the exposed Bastion.   They are also at work near the Mill, and appear to occupy a house between that and the Knoll, nearer the ruins."   At this time, Maj.-Genl. Picton's Division occupied the town of Celorico and neighbourhood ;—the Guards, Cortica and vicinity ;— the Light Division at Riturina, 3 or 4 miles in front and to the right.

August 20.   The Guards arrive and are quartered here (Celorico). Genl. Picton's Division advance to the village to the left of Marsal de Chao ; the Light Division move to Freixerao ; the Cavalry are encamped in the valley between it and Alverca ; Head Quarters are to move to Alverca ; the Guards were ordered to march there also ; but in the course of the day they were countermanded, and all idea of a forward movement vanishes.

August 21.   Head Qrs. returned to this village (Alverca da Beira).
After dinner Col. Fletcher and I rode to Freixedas, and from thence
with the Marquis of Tweedale to a hill from whence we had a tolerable view of Almeida ; the sun set just as we reached the hill and
prevented our seeing the enemy's works.   Almeida keeps up a
constant fire upon the besiegers.   Mulcaster writes from Guarda,
Aug. 19, that the enemy have completed a parallel from the Mill to
the Knoll, and have begun a zig-zag from about the centre of it.   The
firing continues from the place.   The Col. and Chapman looking out
for Telegraph situations.

August 25.   The Guards move from Celorico to Marsal de Chao.
A party of 13th Lt. Dragoons and Portuguese Cavalry take 2 officers
and 39 Dragoons near Belmonte, the Comdg. Officer and 2 others
only escaping.

This dashing little affair, in which the hitherto-despised Portuguese
cavalry gave a specimen of their mettle, is less known than it
deserves to be.   Capt. Warre, on the staff of Marshal Beresford,
wrote to a friend, under date, Aug. 29,—"Capt. White of 13th
Light Dragoons speaks very highly of the gallantry and good conduct
of Cornet Raymundo Oliveira and the troop of the 4th Cavalry who
charged along with his own troop, and tumbled the mounseers over
in a minute (near Castello Branco).   They attacked 60 French
Cavalry, and without loss of man or horse, took 50 men, 7 corporals,
3 sergeants, 2 officers ; others were killed by the peasantry ; not one
went back to tell the tale."

August 26.   Very heavy firing at Almeida during last night ;
increased in the morning and during the day ; the enemy said to
have begun their 2nd Parallel, and to have opened their Batteries on
the place.

August 27.   An explosion heard in the direction of Almeida last
night.   The firing ceased about 10 o'clock this morning.   Col.
Fletcher and I went to the hill on the left of Freixidas at sunset ;
found everything perfectly quiet in the neighbourhood of Almeida,
and concluded that the Fortress had surrendered.   Upon our return
to Alverca found that Lord Wellington, having come to the same
conclusion, had given orders for the army to retire at daylight.   At
¼ past 9 o'clock a heavy fire recommenced at Almeida and continued
until midnight, in consequence of which the orders for retiring were
suspended.   A violent thunder storm with rain again at dusk.

August 28.   Lord Wellington, Col. Fletcher, etc., rode to the front
at daylight ; no firing heard from Almeida ; the enemy felt about our
videttes with a few cavalry and infantry.   About 10 or 11 o'clock
orders were given for Head Qrs. to move to Celorico.   The Lt. Div.,
and Genl. Picton's, halt in the vicinity of Baracal and Marcial de
Chao ; the Guards in Celorico ; the cavalry at Alverca.   The enemy
entered Freixidas, murdered 3 old men, destroyed the Telegraph,

and soon after retired. A great deal of thunder and lightning all day.

August 29. A French Colonel and 3 men of Massena's *gens d'armes* brought in by the peasants from a village between Fort Conception and Guarda. Went with the Col. to Marsul de Chao and fixed upon the height above the village for the Telegraph to communicate from Alverca to Celorico. I rode on to Alverca and examined the hill to find the most eligible site for a Telegraph. A peasant who escaped from Almeida yesterday afternoon came in and reports that the town did not surrender until Tuesday (Aug. 28) about 10 o'clock ; that the garrison laid down their arms on the Glacis, and were marched as prisoners towards Ciudad Rodrigo ; and that the Magazine in the Castle had blown up and damaged the town considerably. The Lt. Div. move into Celorico and the villages near the bridges ; the Guards and the remainder towards the rear.

The disaster, which had so unexpectedly befallen Almeida, is thus described by Napier :—"This fortress was garrisoned by 4,000 Portuguese regulars and militia under the English Col. Cox. On the morning of Aug. 26th sixty-five pieces of artillery, opening at once, set many houses in flames, which the garrison were unable to extinguish. The counter-fire was however briskly maintained and very little military damage was sustained. Towards evening the cannonade slackened, but just after dark the ground suddenly trembled, the castle bursting into a thousand pieces gave vent to a column of smoke and fire, and with a prodigious noise the whole town sunk into a shapeless ruin ! Treason or accident had caused the magazines to explode, and the devastation was incredible. Further resistance was impossible."

The Governor, Colonel Cox, hoped to have held out notwithstanding, till the allies could succour him ; but his efforts were foiled by treachery, and the expressed determination of the Lieut.-Govr. to hoist the white flag. Accordingly the place capitulated.

The only Portuguese Regt. of regulars amongst the garrison of Almeida was the 24th ; and very conflicting statements have been published as to their conduct after capitulation. Napier says bluntly, "The 24th Portuguese regiment certainly took service with the French in a body. Yet, so easily are men's minds moved by present circumstances, that the greater number deserted again when they saw the allied armies." Lord Londonderry speaks of this in even stronger terms, but how little deserved was his sweeping condemnation will be evident from a consideration of the facts set forth by Southey. He tells us that, " when the Portuguese laid down their arms, they were invited to volunteer into the French service ; but not a man was found base enough to come forward. On the following day, they were tried separately ; and were told, that unless they accepted the alternative that was offered them, they must immediately be marched into France ; and the hardships they would suffer were represented to them in strong terms. Officers and men, with an unanimity which might well have been suspected, agreed then to enlist in the enemy's service. They found means of informing Marshal Beresford that they did this only for the sake of remaining within reach of their own country, and making their escape as soon as possible ; and the truth of this was proved by the numbers who soon rejoined the allied army."

Marshal Beresford immediately issued a general order expressing his strong disapprobation of such conduct ; for the soldiers, he said, some allowance was to be made ; yet he hoped that in future any who fell into the enemy's hands would suffer anything rather than bring a stain upon the national honour. With regard to the officers, however, he declared nothing could excuse conduct so base, so abominable, and so unworthy of the Portuguese name ; they had rendered themselves false and infamous ; and that he should report their conduct to their Prince, that they might be dismissed with ignominy from the service. He at the same time published the names of five officers who, under a proper sense of duty, had refused to dishonour themselves in this manner.

Southey further states that a night had not elapsed before great part both of officers and men were missing, and in less than a fortnight nearly the whole had escaped ;—" the men, instead of deserting, rejoining their countrymen in arms ; the officers, unconscious of having done anything unworthy, presenting themselves to the commander of the first detachment they could reach, in a condition which pleaded for them, exhausted with fatigue and hunger." Further enquiry led Marshal Beresford to mitigate the terms of his censure, and to refer the conduct of these officers to a council of inquiry. Further light confirmatory of the above, is thrown on the matter by our Diarist.

August 30. Got the Telegraph erected at Alverca, at daylight this morning ; it fell down soon after ; but, thro. the assistance of Capt. Bull of the Horse Artly. repaired and replaced it again.

Celorico, August 31. Head Qrs. remain in this town ready to retire upon the advance of the French which is hourly expected. The men belonging to the Militia Regts. at Almeida (the Guarda and Arganil) came in, having billets signed by the Marquis de Alorna (a traitorous Portuguese officer who had taken service with the French on Junot's invasion, and was now on the staff of Marshal Massena) stating that they are to return to their homes and not to take arms again ; they report that some, if not the whole of the regular Regt. there, No. 24, (reported as in " very good order " by Capt. Burgoyne in his Diary) have entered the French service. The governor (Col. Cox) and English were marched as prisoners into Spain.

Sept. 1. The enemy's advanced pickets along our whole front appear to be withdrawn towards their own lines.

Sept. 2. A party of the enemy drove in our Cavalry Piquets from Freixidas and Alverca. Head Qrs. remain in readiness to retire at the shortest notice ; orders given to march to Cia in the morning.

Sept. 3. The French retire from Alverca and Freixidas again. Head Qrs. removed to Gouveia, beautifully situated on a small river, and on the side of a hill at the foot of the Serra de Estrella.

Head Qrs. remained here from the 3rd till 16th Sept. Napier thus explains the inactivity of the enemy :—" Massena, chilled by age and honours, was wasting time. He found it difficult to feed his troops, was disinclined to invade so late in the year, and undecided as to the mode. It was two months since Ciudad Rodrigo fell, Almeida had only resisted ten days, yet the French Army was still behind the Coa. It was not until the 15th that Massena's intentions declared themselves : and he advanced in entire ignorance of the tremendous impediment that had been thrown across his path to Lisbon—his declared goal, and the prize he already considered within his grasp."

The entries in the Diary, during this period, may be thus epitomized :—*Sept. 5th.* Ross gone to Celorico to establish a Telegraphic communication with this place. *7th.* Two deserters report that the army under Massena began to retire towards Salamanca and Valladodid 6 days ago ; rumours prevalent that the French are making a movement on our right. *10th.* The peasants brought in a French Surgeon as prisoner ; he is a most shabby figure, and states that Marshal Massena's Head Qrs. are to be at Pinhel to-morrow. *The 24th Regt. of Portuguese infantry who were taken at Almeida, and who entered into the French service have (with the exception of about 20) all deserted and rejoined us.* (The italics are the Editor's). *12th.* Received Newspapers from England to the 25th July ; filled with erroneous and ridiculous statements in the shape of private letters from the army. *13th.* Goldfinch went to the top of the Serra last night at 11 o'clock, with W. and B. to see the rising of the sun from thence. *14th.* Papers arrived from England ; received a letter from poor Hamilton's mother (Capt. Hamilton, his brother-officer who died at Lisbon).

Sept. 15. Heard this evening that the enemy had advanced in force to Celorico. *16th.* Head Qrs. removed to Cea, about noon. The Divisions of the army begin all to retire. Goldfinch remained at Gouveia with Lt.-Col. Waters* to ascertain what numbers of the enemy pass.

Filiadoza, Sept. 17. Marched from Cea to this place in the afternoon ; the army continues retiring. Col. Fletcher and Chapman set off in the morning to reconnoitre about Ponte de Murcella. Had a

---

* A very active and enterprising " Intelligence Officer."

severe attack of the ague before I quitted Cea ; obliged to lie down immediately upon my arrival here. Heard that part of the enemy's force had crossed the Mondego.

Cortica, Sept. 18. Quitted Filiadoza at daybreak, and proceeded along the main road towards Ponte de Murcella, through Lerosa,—like every place in this part of the country, entirely deserted, the poor peasants flying with what they can carry off in every direction.

Lord Wellington, unable, from the smallness of his force, to stem the flood of invasion, was now retiring upon that " stupendous and impregnable citadel," in front of Lisbon, which his forethought had caused to be raised ; while the more effectually to thwart the enemy's designs, he had induced the Portuguese authorities to order the inhabitants along the line of invasion to destroy their mills, remove their boats, break down their bridges, lay waste their fields, abandon their dwellings, and carry away their property. " It was a design of terrible energy "—as Napier truly observes ; that it was not literally carried out, need cause no surprise ; for—as Napier does well to remind us,—" Wellington was a foreigner, ill-supported by his own Government, and holding power under that of Portugal by a pre‐carious tenure ; and he was vehemently opposed by the local authorities, by the ministers, and by the nobility." Moreover, Massena, on the eve of his invasion, had issued a proclamation to the Portuguese, in which he informed them that the Emperor of the French bore them no enmity ;—" on the contrary, it is his highest wish to promote your happiness, and the first step for securing it is to dismiss from the country those locusts who consume your property, blast your harvests, and palsy your efforts " ; and he went on to assure them that " in opposing the Emperor, you oppose your true friend ; a friend who has it in his power to render you the happiest people in the world." But the conduct of the French troops in the course of two previous invasions proved the worthlessness of the Emperor's professions of friendship, and had excited against them feelings of utter detestation.

Reverting to the Diary :—

Sept. 19. *Cortica.* The army began to move towards and across the Mondego, it being ascertained that the main body of the enemy are in Viseu and its neighbourhood. Capt. Mulcaster ordered to pro-ceed with B.-Genl. Pack's Brigade to destroy the bridge near San Combadao and to prepare that at Criz. Lt. Thomson went to destroy the bridge at Taboa. Capt. Burgoyne ordered to Coimbra to report upon the bridge there and wait for orders respecting it. Capt. Chapman reconnoitred part of the position near Moita. The Col. accompanied Lord Wellington on a reconnaissance the other side of the Mondego.

Sept. 20. Passed thro. Ponte de Murcella to Val de Mayor where I was seized with a fit of the ague and was obliged to lie down in a

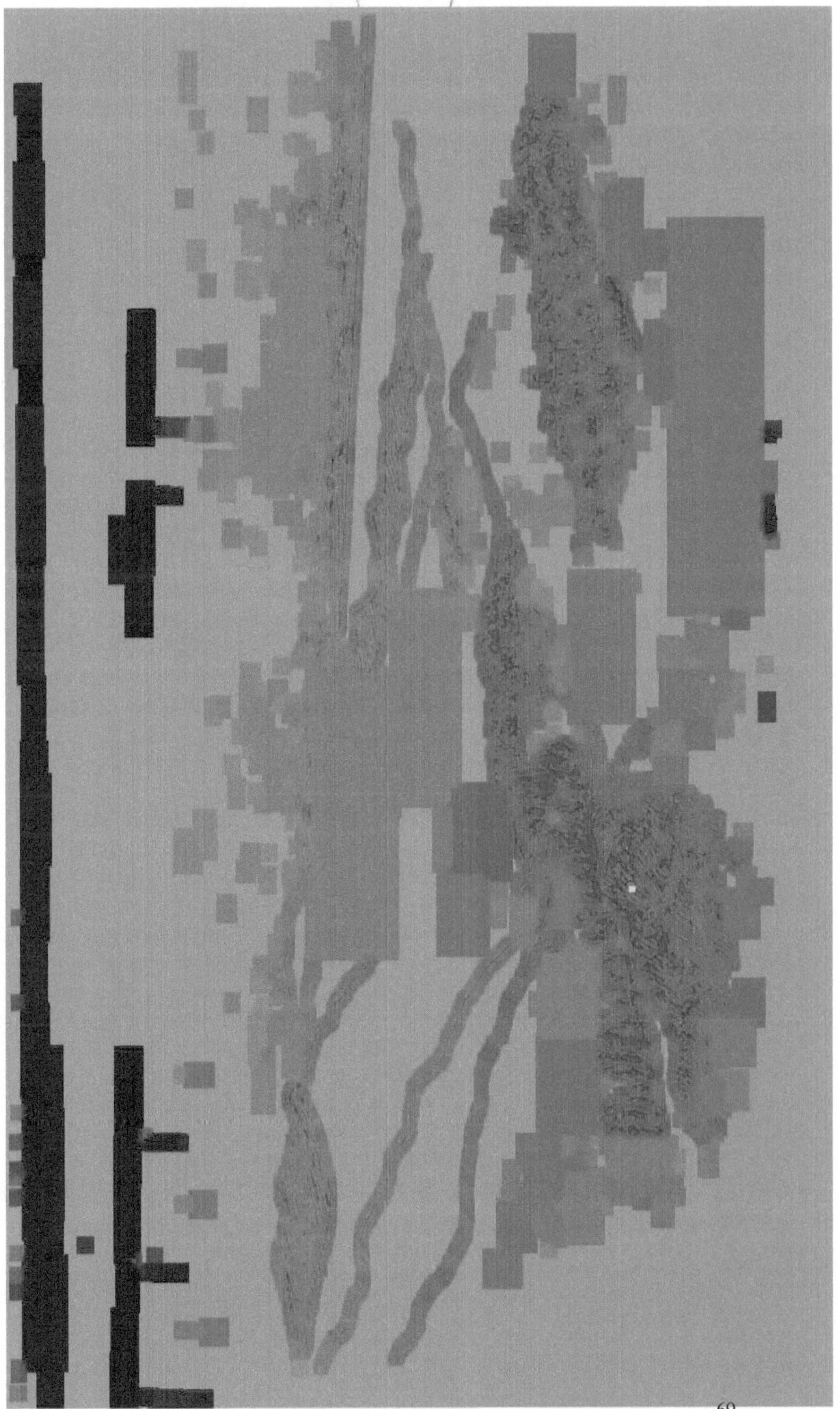

cottage 2 or 3 hours before I could proceed. We crossed the Mondego
at the ford below Pena Cova ; with much difficulty I arrived at
Lurvao.   Quartered in a tolerable house with civil people and
procured good beds.

Sept. 21st, 22nd, 23rd, 25th.   Marched from Lurvao to the Convent
of Bussaco.   Head Qrs. occupied the whole of the Convent* ; the
Departs. attached to Hd. Qrs. are in the little Chapels which are
scattered about the grounds round the Convent. We are in that of
Calvary on the hill overlooking the country north of Coimbra.   Took
my Qrs. in the adjacent little cell of the Hermitage of the Sepulchre,
where I remained for the most part within doors during the five days
mentioned on the margin ; being so ill and weak from the ague that
I was unable to go out ; our officers were busily employed in forming
communications along the position in the Serra, and making a Flèche
for musketry on the left.   On the afternoon of the 25th, the enemy
advanced upon Mortagao and drove our advance into the position,
taking up their own ground on the opposite hill.   Hoey of the
Adjt.-Genl.'s Depart. severely wounded whilst looking out in the front.

Note.—In respect of scenic effect, and grandeur of its surroundings,
probably no military spectacle was ever more superbly staged than
that witnessed by the allied troops, from "grim Busaco's iron ridge"
on the afternoon of Sept. 25th, 1810, while the French Army was
taking up its position on the ground facing, but rather below, that
occupied by the allies. "My regiment had no sooner piled arms,"
wrote Capt. Sherer, "than I walked to the verge of the mountain on
which we lay, in the hope that I might discover something of the
enemy.   Little, however, was I prepared for the magnificent scene
which burst on my astonished sight.   Far as the eye could reach, the
glittering of steel, and clouds of dust raised by cavalry and artillery,
proclaimed the march of a countless army ; thousands of them were
already halted in their bivouacs, and column after column, arriving in
quick succession, reposed upon the ground allotted to them, and
swelled the black and enormous masses.   Here lay before me the
men who had once, for nearly two years, kept the whole coast of
England in alarm ; who had conquered Italy, overrun Austria,
shouted victory on the plains of Austerlitz, and humbled, in one day,
the power, the pride, and the martial renown of Prussia, on the field
of Jena."   To this inspiring description there is appended, in a pencil
note, by an unknown reader :—"Scarcely a dust, as the movements
were executed either on grass or on heath.   I remember it as if I had

* As late as the year 1844, the Prior, leading an English visitor into a
long hall, from whence many cells opened, said to him, "Here, before
the battle your great Duke established his quarters; in that room he
slept; see, I have painted the name of 'Wellington' over the door."

(Now converted into a sumptuous Hotel, and advertised as one of the
"Beauty-spots" of Portugal.   At the time in question, the vast enclosure
was a *terra incognita*).

seen it but yesterday—the vast square bodies of infantry supposed to
contain nearly twenty-thousand men each ;—when they took their
ground it seemed as if they would have kept ranging for ever. . . .
Numbers of fires—the fires of the two armies, making the night one
of the grandest sights I ever saw,—and was, during the whole time
they were opposed to each other." Even Napier admits that, " only
veterans tired of war could have slept while that serene sky glittered
above, and the dark mountains were crowned with the innumerable
bivouac fires of more than a hundred thousand warriors."

Reverting to the Diary :—

Sept. 26. The whole line under arms before daylight this morning.
The fog was for some time very thick ; when it cleared we perceived
the enemy upon the opposite hills ; but they did not attack us during
the day ; remained on the ground until dark.

Sept. 27. The enemy attacked our position soon after 6 o'clock
this Morning, in two strong columns. One attempted to push up the
road to the Convent, but were repulsed as they reached the brow of
the hill, principally by the Light Division. The other at first succeeded in gaining the summit near where the road from St. Antonio
de Cantara to Coimbra crosses the mountain, but were soon driven
back. General St. Simon and 300 men taken ; about 2,000 left on
the ground, and from 5 to 6,000 wounded is the loss of the French.
We lost not more than 200 killed and 1,000 wounded. *The Portuguese astonished us by their coolness and bravery, more particularly
their Cacadores, (Light troops)*. (The italics are the Editor's).

The Battle of Bussaco is wont to be regarded as a British victory.
It must come as an unpleasant surprise, therefore, to many people to
learn that but half of Wellington's army, on that memorable occasion,
was composed of British troops. In the first place there was a con-
tingent of Germans—chiefly Hanoverians—known as the " King's
German Legion," a body of soldiers who rendered invaluable service
throughout the war. But the battle was chiefly notable for the
participation therein of Marshal Beresford's newly-organized Portuguese army, of which over 20,000 men were lined up with the British
troops, for the first time, to give battle to the French invaders. That
is a feature of the battle our writers are too prone to ignore. It is
well to bear in mind, moreover that in default of those brave soldiers
Wellington would never have offered battle. All hope of effective
assistance from the Spaniards had long been abandoned. The
number of British troops available was insignificant. The Portuguese
were the last hope ; everything hinged therefore on their conduct.
Would they face the French ? The opponents of the war, in England,
had scouted the notion of Portuguese levies facing the veterans of
Austerlitz ; and it must be frankly confessed that, amongst the
generality of British officers at the seat of war, there was a feeling of
utter scepticism concerning the fighting qualities of the Portuguese—

S. Vincente Chapel.
Ancient Moorish Castle.
Soccorro Signal Station.
Town of Torres Vedras.

a view differing but little, indeed, from that expressed by Massena in
a letter to the Emperor, before the battle—that they were "a *canaile*
who would bolt at the first shot." The hour had arrived when the
mettle of the Portuguese troops was to be put to the test. And,
naturally, profound anxiety was felt as to the issue. If they turned
their backs on the invader, all hopes of saving Portugal must be
abandoned, and the British troops withdrawn from the country. So
completely had the English Government given up all hope of success,
that, at this very time an officer of Engineers had arrived at Lisbon,
whose instructions,—received personally from Lord Liverpool, commenced thus :—"As it is probable the army will embark in September."* The transports were lying in the Tagus.

In the battle, the Portuguese bore themselves nobly ; winning
ungrudging praise from all who witnessed their behaviour ; and
proving themselves worthy of fighting alongside the troops of their
"ancient ally." Lord Wellington, in his despatch, paid a generous
tribute to the gallantry of the Portuguese, concluding with these
memorable words :—"They have proved that they are worthy of
contending in the same ranks with British troops in this interesting
cause, which they afford the best hopes of saving." Perhaps the
highest compliment paid to the Portuguese troops on that memorable day was by the French General Simon, who, after being taken
prisoner, remarked, that it had been a clever ruse dressing up English
soldiers in Portuguese uniforms, in order to deceive the French.

It was certainly a novel experience for Napoleon's veterans—who
had been accustomed to "walk through" the best troops of the
Continent—to meet with such a drubbing as they had received—
administered, too, by less than half their own numbers. And what
made the pill all the more nauseous was that, of the allied troops
who had administered the drubbing, quite half were the despised
Portuguese—the "*canaile* that would bolt at the first shot ! "

The Battle of Bussaco, viewed in its true perspective, stands out as
the turning-point of the Peninsular War. The opinion had widely
prevailed hitherto, that a few weeks would see the wreck of the
British Army on board its transports in the Tagus. Bussaco had
changed everything. The British troops, according to their wont,
had behaved nobly. But Bussaco taught the world something infinitely more important than that oft-repeated lesson "The day gave
the Portuguese confidence in themselves and with the army in
general," as a British cavalry officer expressed it. It was the right

* A distinguished German, discussing the spirit of pessimism which at
one time prevailed in England, as to the outcome of the struggle,
wrote :—"Why are the English so gloomy in their forebodings of the
issue of this war ?—Because their happy constitution, combined with
English spleen, engenders in them a peculiar foolish tendency, and
makes them the greatest calumniators of themselves. The Briton dis-
parages himself, ignores his own merits, exaggerates his deficiencies,
and is always ringing the alarm-bell."

interpretation of this lesson that enabled Wellington to stem the flood of invasion at the Lines of Torres Vedras, and thence to march, from victory to victory, until, four years later, he was able to dictate terms of peace to the tyrant of Europe on French soil.

It was on that glorious field that the Portuguese began that companionship-in-arms which lasted till the close of the war. Had they shown their backs to the foe on that fateful day—as was foretold, aye, and hoped for by the opposition in England—the Peninsula must have been abandoned forthwith.

What were Lord Wellington's views in respect of the battle? Writing, a few days afterwards to the Rt. Hon. W. Pole, he observes :—" The croakers about useless battles will attack me again on that of Bussaco, *notwithstanding that our loss was really trifling : but I should have been inexcusable if, knowing what I did, I had not endeavoured to stop the enemy then,* and I should have stopped him entirely if it had not been for the blunders of the Portuguese General commanding in the North, who was prevented by a small French patrol from sending Trant up the road by which he was ordered to march. If he had come by that road, the French could not have turned our position, and they must have attacked us again : they could not have carried it and they must have retired. . . . To this add that the battle has had the best effects in inspiring confidence in the Portuguese troops, both among our croaking officers and the people of the country. This likewise removed an inference which began to be very general, that we intended to fight no more, but to retire to our ships : and it has given the Portuguese troops a taste for an amusement to which they were not before accustomed, and which they would not have acquired if I had not put them in a very strong position."

Bussaco, Sept. 28. Remained under arms all day; the enemy appear to be making a number of movements, that end in their turning our left flank, and obliging us to retire, which we did in the night by torch-light, and in great confusion.

A night-retirement, by torch-light, through the Convent woods, over the rough, precipitous tracks—hardly deserving the name of roads—in the rear, would naturally entail some confusion. And this is confirmed by Capt. Burgoyne, of the Engineers, who was attached to Picton's Division. Orders for retirement were only received at 1 a.m., on the 29th :—" It was a rainy night, the road was very bad, and we found much confusion in Genl. Leith's part of the line . . . some regimental pickets not called in, etc. . . . Our pickets which were to have retired in a body at daylight, finding this confusion, did not march off till 8 ; they destroyed 36 barrels of ammunition found in the rear of Genl. Leith's ground, and recommended a Portuguese Regt. of Militia which was on the heights, *and had received no orders,* to retire."

CHAPTER SEVEN

Coimbra, Sept. 29, 1810.   Went from Bolao to Fornas to find Col.
Fletcher ; dined there with Lord Wellington and Marshal Beresford ;
the former gave me a letter for the Col. which I took to Coimbra in
the evening.   Head Qrs. were at Coimbra on the 30th.   Next
morning,—" suddenly, obliged to leave Coimbra at about 8 o'clock ;
the roads crowded to excess with fugitives of all ranks, ages and
sexes ; Head Qrs. established at Condexa ; soon after, ordered to
proceed to Redinha, where we arrived by the evening."

Oct. 2.   Leiria.   Marched with Head Qrs. from Redinha ; roads
crowded with inhabitants from the country we retire from.

NOTE.—The enforced migration of the inhabitants entailed
appalling distress and confusion, and, naturally, hampered the movements of the troops.   The misery, indeed, caused by this exodus far
exceeded anything witnessed in the course of Sir John Moore's retreat
on Corunna ; and, with the arrival of Wellington's troops at Coimbra
a climax was reached.   The sufferers, be it remembered, too, were
peaceful citizens, who, the year before, had welcomed these very
troops with frantic enthusiasm as their deliverers ; but who now
beheld them, flying before the victorious hosts of the great Napoleon.
The horrors that were crowded into the next few weeks have,
probably, never been exceeded.   Even our own historians have felt
compelled to gloss over the sickening tale.   Nevertheless, we may
obtain a fairly adequate notion of the scenes enacted along all the
roads converging on Lisbon, by a search through the masses of long-
forgotten war-literature, wherein, amidst much that is of purely
antiquarian or professional interest, we, ever and anon light on
descriptions which, for realistic power and gruesome interest, might
vie with the word-paintings of some of our most accomplished " war
correspondents " of the present day.   A perusal of the pages of
Napier, Lord Londonderry, Tomkinson, and others would prove a
veritable revelation to those of our countrymen who are prone to
regard the Peninsular War as a mere record of British military
exploits, without attempting to realize the frightful sufferings that
struggle entailed on the innocent inhabitants of the land.

Leiria. Oct. 3. The troops plundered this place dreadfully ; some of those taken in the act, hung directly ; the inhabitants having all fled.

NOTE.—These acts of plunder drew from Lord Wellington the following General Order :—" The Commander of the Forces is concerned to have been under the necessity of carrying into execution the determination which he has so long announced, of directing the immediate execution of any soldiers caught plundering. Two soldiers, a British and a Portuguese, have been hanged this day for plundering in the town of Leyria. He trusts that this example will deter others from these disgraceful practices in future. The troops are well fed and taken care of, and there is no excuse for plunder."—LEYRIA, Oct. 3, 1810.

Alcobaca. Oct. 5. Marched with Head Qrs. to this place ; found the houses quite deserted ; procured a good qrs. Light Division occupy Batalha.

NOTE.—As this was the last occasion, on which the monks of these two splendid Monasteries—Alcobaca being one of the richest in Europe—were able to dispense hospitality to British soldiers, before suffering destruction and shameful sacrilege at the hands of the invaders, the following quotation from Capt. J. Burgoyne's Diary will be acceptable :—

Oct. 3. " At Batalha is a very large and rich Convent of Monks. The whole British Regts. of this Division (Picton's) were quartered in it easily ; as well as the Generals and many other officers. Several Divisions of the British Army had, at various times, passed thro. this place, and some remained several days, during all which time a dinner was prepared at the Convent for the whole of the officers. On this day (Oct. 3, 1810) it was done for the last time, at least for the present, for the greater part of the Friars had already left the Convent, and the remainder quitted it this evening. They had had a ship prepared at St. Martino, for some time before, to take them off with their plate and most valuable effects. They leave a quantity of hay, straw, vegetables, etc., which they beg the General to distribute, as if not, the French will have it."

Junot, and his soldiers—whom we conveyed back to France, in British ships, under the terms of the Convention of Cintra—had already skimmed the cream from the Church treasures of Portugal, and thus given a pretty plain inkling of the sort of treatment to be meted out to ecclesiastical property, in future.

Returning to the Diary :—

Oct. 6. Marched with Head Qrs. to this place (Rio Major). Delancy procured me a tolerable Qrs.

Oct. 7. Marched alone on a foggy morning ; got a good Qrs. on the hill at Alemquer.

Oct. 8. Ordered to Arruda in the afternoon ; a very wet march ; my baggage pony left on the road.

Oct. 9. Very rainy ; Lord Wellington went to Torres Vedras. Good Qrs. (Arruda) abundance of grapes and wine.

Oct. 10. San Quintana. This is the most miserable village we were ever quartered in. Rain continues.

NOTE.—The Allied troops were now taking up position behind the Lines ; a few words of explanation with reference to this movement, and the state and condition of those great defensive works, may therefore prove acceptable. And first, it may be well to draw attention to the secrecy with which the labour on the Lines had been carried on,— over a great extent of country, and during a period of eleven months. True, silence with respect to the nature and extent of the works was strictly enjoined on all engaged ; and, with the exception of a bare notification in certain English Newspapers, early in 1810, that men were employed in fortifying the position, no further information leaked out. Yet, as Southey justly remarks, the circumstance of works of such magnitude and importance having been commenced and perfected without attracting the slightest attention during their progress is without a parallel in history. To the present generation, —with its hordes of " Reporters "—intent on getting " copy " by fair means or by foul—the keeping of the secret must seem incomprehensible.

Napier tells us that " only vague rumours of their existence " reached the bulk of the English Army ; and that neither the Portuguese Government, nor the British envoy, knew their nature ; they imagined the entrenchments round Lisbon were the Lines. It is possible that, had Wellington's officers being better informed on the subject, there would have been less despondency with respect to the issue of the campaign. The works, when completed, consisted of three distinct lines of defence, of which the second was the most important and by far the strongest ; the first being designed merely as a sort of advanced position to stem the tide of invasion while the Army was taking post on the second without hurry or confusion ; while the third was a mere place of refuge, to cover the point of embarkation at the Tagus mouth. The determination to abide the attack in the first was an after-thought.

During the last few months, work on the Lines had been pushed on at high pressure ; with the result that, on Oct. 6, just previous to the arrival of the advance-guard of the army, the Superintending Engineer (Capt. J. T. Jones, who had been left in charge of the works after Col. Fletcher joined Lord Wellington at Celorico) was able to report that " every preparation for an instant defence of the lines is now complete, and you need be under no apprehension for our credit, even if the enemy attack as the rear division enters the works . . . the powder is in the cases to load the mines, and the officers, each in his own district, is prepared to meet the divisions. . . . Now everything is in confusion ; the people are all running away ; and a string of men, women, and children in cars, on animals, and on foot,

are crowding every road to Lisbon. No one will believe that the
army will halt till it reaches St. Julian's (at the Tagus mouth) and all
authority and order is beginning to be lost."

The following saying had been current, for some time past :—" The
Portuguese are for the land, the English for the sea ! "

How suggestive is the concluding paragraph of Capt. Jones' report :—
" When I heard of the Bussaco business, I began to be alarmed for the
consequences of having done so much ; for if the lines had not come
into play the expense would most likely have been cavilled at as unnecessary ; but now, of course, only the benefit derived from the
strength of the works will be considered. I flatter myself you will be
much pleased with the quantity of work of every nature done since
your departure."

As the ground was strange to the several Divisions—the very
existence of the Lines being unknown to the officers commanding—
Lord Wellington, with his wonted foresight, had given instructions for
the Engineer officers who had been engaged on the works to be told
off as guides. Thus Col. Fletcher writes from Alcobaca, Oct. 5, to
Capt. Jones ;—" Lord Wellington has directed me to write to you on
the subject of guides for the different districts of our works," and
after naming the officers for the duties and desiring that they might
be at the Head Qrs. of the several districts, he adds that,—" Lord
Wellington wishes that an officer of the ordenanzas, or any other
respectable person well qualified from local knowledge, should be
appointed, with about four men under him, also well qualified, to
show the roads from the works along the positions, and those leading
to them from the front. . . . The officers and a part of the men
must be mounted. . . . I am sure you will make every arrangement for this service immediately. . . . I would recommend that
the men should be constantly practised in acquiring every information
about the roads of and bordering on the several districts. Every
possible preparation is now of course necessary towards the defence
of our works."

On the 8th Oct. amidst torrential rain—fit accompaniment of the
pitiful scenes enacted along the lines of retreat, and which continued
for several days, without intermission—the allied troops entered the
positions prepared for them ; the several Divisions being shep-
herded by the guides into their respective stations ; nevertheless
a good deal of confusion ensued in some parts, from unavoidable
causes.

At this critical juncture, Lord Wellington's plans were suddenly
altered to meet the exigencies of the situation. The army entered
the Lines, with the expectation of taking up ground on the main, or
second defensive position, in order to dispute—according to Sir John
Jones, than whom no officer in the army was better informed of the
Chief's intentions—the principal passes of Mafra, Montachique,

Bucellas, etc.*   But the movements of the troops not being pressed by
the enemy—and the soldiers of both nationalities being animated with
an excellent spirit, in consequence of the victory at Bussaco—an
embarrassment was felt about the positions entrenched at Torres
Vedras and Monte Agraca, etc., along the first line.   To have abandoned those formidable works without a shot being fired would have
produced the worst possible effects, not on the populace alone, but
upon the troops.   Consequently, Lord Wellington, aware of the great
strength these advanced positions had attained, decided to halt at
Sobral, and there abide the attack.

Reverting to the Diary :—

San Quintana, Oct. 11.   This morning we were turned out of our
poor Qrs. : regained it again.   Dined at Lord Wellington's.

NOTE.—It was from here, on this very day, that Lord Wellington
wrote to General Craufurd :—"Sta. Quintina, near Sobral, half-past
11 a.m.   I hope that your men are well put up in Arruda in this
terrible weather   .   .   ."   And next day he writes to Mr. Stuart :—
"No tents arrived yet ; the troops are suffering everywhere for
want of them."   And to General Pack :—"In respect to tents, the
Portuguese Government were to supply them, but they have failed
in this, as they have in everything else."

Arranhol, Oct. 12.   Head Qrs. moved here from St. Quintana.
Sent from the fort of Sobral to mine a road below Zibreira, which
occupied all night ;—the party from the Guards.   *Oct.* 13.   Met Lord
Wellington on my way back this morning, after being relieved ;
ordered back to see the mine exploded, and to get powder from
the German Artillery.

Oct. 15.   Head Qrs. moved to Enxara dos Cavaleiros.   Our Qrs.
robbed in the evening ; Chapman lost a portfolio with sketches, Col.
Fletcher his dressing articles.   Rode up to the Fort of Monte Agraça
by daylight every morning, when both armies are under arms on their
respective positions.

Oct. 17.   *Pero Negro.*   Arrived in this wretched village where it is
said Head Qrs. are to be established.   No good Qrs. except Lord
Wellington's and the Adjt.-Genl.'s.   Lived very well by sending to
Lisbon for supplies, but much harassed by turning out before daylight
every morning.

* The author of *Wellington's Lieutenants* could scarcely have been aware
of this when he cast a slur on the professional reputation of a distinguished
Engineer Officer, by stating that the Pass of Matos, " apparently had been
unaccountably overlooked by Fletcher, who had superintended the fortifications " (page 152, General Craufurd).   Had he consulted Sir John
Jones' work on the Lines of Torres Vedras, he would have learned that
the troops were employed continuously in completing and strengthening
the position, which, at the last moment, Wellington had decided on
holding.

Note.—From the date above-named, until Nov. 5th, when Jones was detached to Lisbon on other duties, there are no entries in the Diary. The blank may be fittingly filled in by a quotation from Sir John Jones' History :—"Every morning, two hours before daybreak, the troops stood to their arms at the point of assembly of their several cantonments, as did also the garrisons of the several works ; Lord Wellington, in person, being in the fort of Monte Agraça, in readiness to direct any general movement. The weather was generally wet, and the duty irksome ; still, all supported it with cheerfulness, in the full confidence of annihilating their opponent, whenever the threatened attack should take place ; but after a week had elapsed, expectation could no longer support itself, and the hope of an immediate and brilliant triumph subsided."

Lord Wellington, in a letter to the Earl of Liverpool, dated Oct. 27, 1810, wrote—"I am not quite certain that I ought not to attack the French . . . but I think the sure game, and that in which I am likely to lose the fewest men, the most consistent with my instructions and the intentions of the King's Government ; and I therefore prefer to await the attack."

The condition of the French *vis-à-vis* of the Lines was deplorable. Massena had followed leisurely in the wake of the allied army, without stores, and short of provisions, buoyed up with the prospects of enjoying the plunder of Lisbon, which wealthy city he reckoned as already within the grasp of his troops. When, therefore, he found his path blocked by the impregnable Lines of Torres Vedras—of whose very existence he had been unaware—he must have experienced a rude shock. As time went on, the situation of his troops becoming desperate, retreat was inevitable.

From this check in front of the Lines may be dated the decline of French power. As Sir J. Jones truly observes :—"It was the first and only instance of a military enterprise planned and matured by Napoleon, whilst in the plenitude of his power, being defeated by the steady perseverance and superior foresight of an opponent."

To return to the Diary :—

Nov. 5. Set out from Pero Negro this morning, being ordered to assist Capt. Goldfinch in reconnoitring the left bank of the Tagus opposite Lisbon and the Peninsula between Aldea Gallega and Setubal.

Note.—This expedition was connected with certain defensive works, rendered necessary by a report from the Admiral commanding in the Tagus to the effect that, owing to the increasing number of ships in the river, they would be liable to destruction from the fire of the enemy, in the event of his seizing the heights on the south side. Lord Wellington, in his reply to Admiral the Hon. G. Berkeley, wrote :—"It is quite clear to me that Portugal and England cannot afford a force to do more than defend one side of the river ; and if

the transports cannot remain in safety, the enemy being in possession
of the left bank, the defence of the country ought not to be attempted.
. . . I am perfectly aware of the strength of the ground on the
left of the Tagus . . . and I have reports and plans for fortifying
and occupying it, but I have never thought of carrying the plans into
execution for the reasons I have above stated."

As matter of fact, certain defensive works, together with roads of
communication, were subsequently constructed along the heights on
the south bank, as shown on the plans attached to Sir John Jones'
account of the Lines.

Messrs. Goldfinch and Jones having reconnoitred the ground,
returned to Lisbon on Nov. 10th. *Lisbon, Nov.* 15. The French
retired to Santarem last night. (During the next 3 weeks Jones
remained in Lisbon ; Col. Fletcher and various officers being engaged,
from time to time, in superintending work on the south bank of the
Tagus).

It may be of interest here to mention a circumstance which seems
to have escaped the notice of historians namely, that Lord Cochrane,
who was on board his yacht, the *Julie*—originally a small French
warship which had been captured, and afterwards bought by this
officer—in the Tagus, when the troops entered the Lines (Oct., 1810)
with his accustomed zeal,—although on half-pay at the time, volunteered to go up the river and destroy all the French boats at Santarem.

From Capt. J. Burgoyne, Royal Engineers.

Cartaxo, 20th Nov., 1810.

My Dear Jones,

I cannot do less than write you the news in return for the letters I
received from you on your first joining the army. Head Qrs. have been
here for these three days past ; it was understood that the greater part
of the French Army had crossed the Zezere, and that only 5 Regiments
were left in Santarem ; under that impression an attack was intended
yesterday. The French force is posted in rear of the Causeway about
two miles from Santarem ; and they have their artillery posted to fire
along that approach. It was therefore arranged that General Pack should
turn their right, and the light brigade their left. General Pack's Division
arrived in good time at the ford or causeway by which it was intended he
should cross the valley ; but the Artillery and Dragoons intended for his
support mistook the road ; the latter did not arrive until very late, and
the former did not reach him during the day. General Pack having
observed two Battalions posted with four Cannon on the opposite side to
oppose his passage, deemed it proper to send to Lord W. to know if he
should attempt it without his guns. All this created delay, and at 3 o'clock
it was judged too late to attempt anything that day. It is said that in the
evening His Lordship received information that the bulk of the French
Army is on this side the Zezere, and in consequence determined to substi-
tute a false attack for the real one, and to see if the enemy could be

frightened enough by it to give up the hill defending the causeway, and
retire into Santarem. All the usual demonstrations were made this
morning; the different columns were put into motion, and the light troops
skirmished absolutely into the rear of the post; but devil a bit did a
Frenchman move from his ground. It is therefore concluded that the
enemy is in force at Santarem, and as we do not deem ourselves strong
enough to carry a small advanced post, an attack upon Santarem itself
cannot be for a moment expected. I therefore think we shall remain here
until Massena is reinforced, when we shall again return to Pero Negro.
I have made up my mind to a daily wetting. I will thank you to send the
accompanying letter for Ross to the Portuguese Post Office. Saturday
is Mafra post day.

Believe me, yours very faithfully.

J.B.

I am nearly out of Horse Shoe Nails; if you will send me up a few I shall
be very thankful to you. Your horse is come quite round, and I expect
will be in very fair riding order in ten days or a fortnight.

Dec. 16. After inspecting the Bridge of Mealhada, (Ponte de Rio
Georgo) with Col. Fletcher, consisting of 3 small arches over the
Rio Mayor, began a mine, with a party of the Guards. *Dec.* 25.
Completed the Mine and loaded it with a Barrel and a half of powder.
Returned to dinner (Xmas Day) and just sitting down to it with the
Brigade Major, when the Col. came from Lord Wellington's where he
was to dine, to desire the bridge in the Causeway leading to Santarem
to be mined immediately. Sent the mules with some intrenching
tools, eat my dinner and set out for the Bridge. Waited from half-
past 8 till 10 o'clock for a party, during which time I rode to
Genl. Craufurd's Qrs. who was dining out. Procured a few men from
the inlying picket commanded by Capt. Jones of the 52nd Regt.
Began about midnight; although close to the abattis that separated
our sentries from the French, and the noise reverberated on the arch,
the enemy gave us little interruption. Brig.-Major Jones relieved me
at 4 o'clock, and completed the mine soon after light.

Cartaxo. Dec. 26. Sent to the left of our position on the Rio
Major, and mined a small bridge of one arch; could obtain only
9 in. in depth. Loaded it with 60 Six-pounder Cartridges. Lost my
way in the darkness and intricate by-roads, with a dragoon that
accompanied me, till daylight.

Dec. 30. At Major Sturgeon's suggestion an attempt was made to
dam the Rio Major, by filling the arches of Ponte St. Anna with wine
casks.

THE WINTER OF 1810–11.

Behind the Lines.—The influx of such a host of destitute and starving creatures—almost the entire population of a province and the
principal inhabitants of Coimbra and other towns,—raised the gravest

apprehensions in Lisbon. The number of refugees that had to be cared for during the winter of 1810—1811, was estimated at three hundred thousand, irrespective of about one hundred and twenty thousand troops. And the task of providing food and shelter for this immense multitude was a gigantic one. Yet it was accomplished. All classes united in the endeavour to mitigate the sufferings of the poor creatures to the utmost of their power ;—" everything which prudence and humanity could suggest," wrote an eye-witness, " was done by the inhabitants of Lisbon to alleviate the public misfortune. Charitable institutions were set on foot, and food was daily distributed to such of the fugitives as were necessitous and helpless, while labour was provided for the others." Nor was the British nation backward in showing sympathy for its "ancient ally." The officers of Lord Wellington's army contributed liberally out of their private means ; while at home, the House of Commons voted for the relief of the poor sufferers a sum of one hundred thousand pounds; a sum at least equal to this being raised by voluntary subscription ; and the money was very judiciously employed in the purchase and freightage of such things in Great Britain as the Portuguese were most immediately in want of.

" The misery and wretchedness of the refugees is beyond description," wrote Capt. Dickson (Sir A. Dickson) of the Portuguese Artillery, (Feb. 28, 1811) ; " numbers are perishing from disease and want. A very handsome subscription was made by the British Division for the poor at Chamesca, but, alas, it is all gone, and the streets (in Chemesca) are as full of misery as ever. It is quite melancholy to see the state of the poor people ; women are to be seen in all directions gathering herbs which they cook and nearly live on."

Later on, after the expulsion of the invaders, a large additional sum of money was sent from England, with a view to resettling the peasantry on their derelict farms ; and a joint commission, partly British and partly Portuguese, was engaged for several months in examining claims and apportioning the awards.

And so Lisbon was saved, and with it the cause of European freedom. But at what frightful cost the world will never know. Great Britain still bears the burden of that tremendous contest in her National Debt.

And how did the inhabitants of the Portuguese metropolis bear themselves under the strain of that terrible winter ? After the first few weeks a reaction set in ; the people as it were, became intoxicated with a strong feeling of security :—" There never was a period," wrote an eye-witness, " when this city was crowded with more objects of misery ; yet at no time had their theatres been better filled, their societies more gay and brilliant, than when seventy thousand vindictive enemies lay within sixteen miles of the city, panting for the plunder of it."

The following statement might seem incredible were it not made on the authority of General Cockburn, who wrote :—" Last winter, when there was great distress in Lisbon, and men were absolutely starving, public offers were made of rations and 6d. a day to any man who would work on the Lines ; yet the majority preferred an existence on casual charity, and basking in the sun, to the above wages and work. The French," he adds, " took a much shorter and better plan ; they gave no money and forced them to work."

Before the Lines.—The condition of the French Army, during this terrible winter, was unspeakably wretched ; but no amount of suffering could palliate their savage treatment of the innocent inhabitants of a country they had, avowedly, entered to protect.

Perhaps the most realistic and terrible description of the barbarities practiced by Massena's troops during this awful period, is that touched on by Southey, in his History of the War. With a profounder knowledge of Portuguese history than any foreigner, and excellent source of information at command, he takes us behind the scenes, and affords us glimpses of what was taking place in the rear of the French position. One or two extracts from this little-studied work will enable the reader to realize in some faint degree the sufferings of the unfortunate Portuguese during this most terrible crisis. Describing the French marauding parties, Southey tells us that "they were soon left to take their course, without the slightest attempt at restraint. . . . In excuse for this, the French officers observe, and truly, that the army must otherwise have perished.

"The skill which some of these marauders acquired in their search for food, resembled the sagacity with which savages track their prey. That they should detect with unerring certainty any place of concealment in a dwelling or an out-house, might have been expected ; but when they were questing in woods, or among rocks, or in the open country, a new sense seemed to be developed in them. There were men in every company who could discover a depôt of provisions by scent far off.

The conditions under which Massena's troops found themselves, during that terrible winter, were doubtless responsible, to a great extent, for their conduct."

Very apposite are the reflections of an officer on the staff of Marshal Beresford :—" How little does the independent, happy English peasant know how to value the peace and security in which he lives !"—wrote Capt. Warre to his father, during the retreat,—" And how would those miscreants who preach discontent and faction through the country, giving them ideas of wants and liberties which are incompatible with society and government—how would they blush if they were to witness the sufferings and oppression which these poor people undergo."

The following order from Lord Wellington was intended to check the writing of alarmist letters by officers and men of the British Army :—

CELORICO, Aug. 10, 1810.

The Commander of the Forces publishes to the army the extract of a letter, conveying enclosures from the Vice Consul at Oporto, and of British officers of rank in the army, exciting alarm in that city.

The Commander of the Forces will not make any enquiry to discover the writer of the letters which have occasioned this unnecessary alarm, in a quarter in which it was most desirable it should not be created. He has frequently lamented the ignorance which has appeared in the opinions communicated in letters written from the army, and the indiscretion with which those letters are published. It is impossible that many officers of the army can have a knowledge of facts to enable them to form opinions of the probable events of the campaign; but their opinions, however erroneous, must have mischievous effects.

The communication of that of which all officers have a knowledge, viz. the number and disposition of the different divisions of the army, and of its magazines, is still more mischievous than the communication of opinions ; as must be obvious to those who reflect that the army has been for months in the same position : and it is a fact, come to the knowledge of the Commander of the Forces, that the plans of the enemy have been founded on information of this description, extracted from English newspapers; which information must have been obtained through private letters from the officers of the army.

Although the difficulties, inseparable from the situation of every army engaged in operations in the field, particularly in those of a defensive nature, are much aggravated by communications of this description, the Commander of the Forces only requests that the officers will, for the sake of their own reputations, avoid to give opinions upon which they cannot have a knowledge to enable them to form any : and that if they chose to communicate facts to their correspondents, regarding the positions of the army, its numbers, formations of its magazines, preparations for breaking bridges, etc., they will urge their correspondents not to publish their letters in the newspapers, until it shall be certain that the publication of the intelligence will not be injurious to the army or to the public service.

1811. Early in January, Jones obtained a short leave to visit Lisbon on business, and put up at the " Lion d'Or." For a description of the principal Lisbon Hotel, we must turn to the narrative of another officer, who is more explicit on the subject, than our Diarist. "Not an inn," he writes, " is to be found in which you could pass the night without undergoing the tortures of hell, almost as bad to me as flames and brimstone. I made an attempt to lodge in one (Lion d'Or) ; but had I been destined to pass my nocturnal hours in the most wretched hovel in England, or to have put up in this place, I should have preferred the former. It would be impossible to find in all Great Britain a habitation so ruinous, so ill-furnished, so filthy, and so infested with vermin as this ; and yet this was the Lion d'Or, the chief hotel in the city."

Cartaxo, *Jan.* 8, 1811.

My Dear Father,

. . . Our Head Qrs. continue in this town and the outposts are situated as I described in my last; and the peace which then appeared to reign between the two hostiles remains uninterrupted. I fancy the French have received the expected reinforcements under General Devoust, but I do not believe they will attempt anything until they get still larger reinforcements.

My friend Capt. Chapman left us about a fortnight ago; I spoke to him previous to his departure respecting the Adjutancy, and I am sure he will do everything in his power for me; but I fear he will arrive too late to profit by Lord Mulgrave's friendship. . . . You know best whether Sir W. is at all disposed to forward my views in life; if he is, I need hardly remind you that the only way an officer of our Corps can get on at all, is by getting something out of the immediate Regimental duty, if possible still under the Ordnance. . . .

You will see by the impression that I have been obliged to get a new seal; my old one was stolen, with (what I regret infinitely more) the watch Sir Watkin was good enough to give me, from the table in my Quarters, which, from the depredations of the French, is without locks and almost without doors.

Your very dutiful and loving son,

Rice Jones.

Later on in January, he paid a visit to his friend Goldfinch, at Almada, on the south side of the Tagus, putting up at his Quinta, and the following day "rode with him along the works he is constructing, and then got him to return to Lisbon with me; met Burgoyne, Ross, etc., and dined together."

Jan. 20. Received an order to take charge of part of the works at Almada whilst waiting for the arrival of the Artificers, (from England); crossed with my horses to Cosilhos (Casilhas or Almada), and from thence went to Nossa Senhora Da Monte, as arranged with Goldfinch, on the right of his line of works; got a good Qrs. and agreed to live with Thomson during my stay.

Jan. 23. From Monday morning (21) to this, employed in getting acquainted with the duty at Almada. In the middle of the day Goldfinch gave me a letter ordering my return to Head Qrs. Crossed over to Lisbon immediately. Heard of the death of the Marquis de la Romana at Cartaxo last night; also of the appearance of a party of French under Junot at Rio Major, on the 19th inst. Junot received a severe wound and they retired during the night.

On Jan. 25th, Jones rejoined Head Qrs.; next day—"rode with Capt. Jones to Alcoentre, and received from him directions for carrying on the works to be erected here. Maj.-Genl. Colville, who commanded here, made me an offer of his house and table during my stay.

Jan. 27. The party finished felling the fir wood. Laid out the embrasures in the Battery above the town.

Jan. 28. Commenced a Fascine manufactory; weather very fine but hot.

Jan. 29. Received at night an order to form 2 abattis, cut Olive-trees, and form a dam.

Feb. 6. Rejoined Head Qrs. Hear that the French broke ground before Badajoz on the 3rd inst.

Cartaxo, Feb. 7. Feeling unwell applied to Dr. Gunning for medicine and advice. Everything continuing quiet; mornings regularly occupied waiting for orders at the Adjt.-Genl.'s; the remainder of the time disposed of by Col. Fletcher, with whom and the Brig.-Major I mess and live very comfortably.

CARTAXO, Feb. 9, 1811.

MY DEAR FATHER,

Nothing of consequence has occurred between the hostile armies since my last. The French entered Rio Major on the 20th Ult., but withdrew from thence the same night, and Junot was severely wounded whilst reconnoitring near that place by one of our videttes. The Marquis de la Romana died in this town a day or two after. I am very glad to tell you that the Spanish Army of 8 or 10,000 men, . . . have returned towards the Spanish frontier, near Badajoz, which Fortress has been completely invested by Mortier's Corps, who broke ground before it on the 3rd Inst.

I have been attached to the left Division (M.-Genl. Picton's) ever since the appearance of the enemy in that direction on the 20th Inst. and have been throwing up a few batteries, cutting down trees, forming abattis, etc.; I was attached to the Honble. M.-Genl. Colville during the time; he was very civil, and I lived at his table constantly; I returned from thence yesterday. The appointment of Brigade Major makes little or no difference to me, as Adjutant; he is, I believe, much my friend, and in every way a sterling character, both as a man and an officer. . . . If I get it (the home appointment), I shall now have the satisfaction of knowing that I do not owe it to any application, or importunity of my own; and if I do not, I shall only have to remain contented, and without feeling particular obligation to any of my friends in office. . . . I fancy the augmentation will be out, and everything arranged before you receive this.

I remain, my dear Father,

Your very affectionate son,
RICE JONES.

March 6. Heard the French had begun to retreat from Santarem last night.

NOTE.—The retreat of the French from Portugal was the inevitable sequel to the events of the past five months. Massena, early in Oct.,

1810, finding his progress blocked by the Lines of Torres Vedras, after fretting in front of them for a month, not daring to assault, and too proud to confess failure, by retreat, placed his troops in winter quarters about Santarem. Thus situated, his army greatly deteriorated—the fruit of indiscipline, want of provisions and supplies of all sorts, to say nothing of despondency, the natural outcome of baffled hopes. Had Wellington possessed the highly-tempered weapon which was subsequently forged, he would assuredly have fallen, tooth and nail, on to the enemy, and driven them a disorganized rabble, across the frontier. But with his hetereogeneous army of four different nationalities, it would have been folly to risk the momentous interests at stake on the issue of a general action. He had no alternative, therefore, but to bide his time. Meanwhile "General Starvation" was working ruin amongst the enemy, whose long-delayed retreat was marked by the most ruthless devastation. Suffice to state that the track of the retreating army was a desert for long after, littered with smoking ruins, amidst which lay the charred corpses of their late occupants—the peasantry of Portugal.*

Massena re-crossed the frontier on the 5th of April. He had entered Portugal, nine months previously, with nearly 70,000 men — veterans who had beaten the best soldiers of the Continent, and who anticipated an easy conquest of Portugal, together with the expulsion of the "English leopard." He repassed the frontier with 45,000—which included 10,000 reinforcements. The campaign had, therefore, cost the French 30,000 men—to say nothing of the enormous loss of reputation resulting from such a calamitous failure. No French army ever again entered Portugal.

The following extract from a Diary is in the handwriting of Rice Jones, and describes Massena's retreat from Portugal.

HEAD QRS., LOUCAO, Saturday, 16 March.
About 1½ Leagues in front of Miranda do Corvo.

Monday, 11*th*. The enemy being still posted in front of Pombal all the troops were brought to that point; by noon they were driven out of the town, having first set it on fire. They then retired to a position in rear of the town and appeared to be from 20 to 25,000 in number; every preparation was made to attack them, but it became so very late before the rear Divisions could be brought up, and most of the men having marched six leagues, the attack was deferred until the morning.

Tuesday, 12*th*. The enemy retired in the night and we did not overtake them till within ¾ of a league of Redinha. They were posted on a height

---

* "When they looked on these scenes of desolation," wrote an eye-witness, "and considered the desecration of everything, whether sacred or profane, their hearts grew sick within them, and they thought of the happy isle which they had left behind, where such horrors are unknown—unknown to the mercantile citizens, who grudge so much the pittance received by the poor soldier."

at the extremity of a heath, having a view of their front of two miles. The country we were marching through was very close and intersected; on their right was a woody hill. Our Light Division were ordered to drive them out of it, whilst our columns were coming up, and which they did in great style. Our columns then deployed into two lines and a Reserve, (35,000 men) and advanced across the heath (being under a considerable cannonade), our guns as usual in front. It was a beautiful sight, every man could be seen at the same time. The enemy could not resist, and were driven down the hills, through Redinha, the guns cutting them up famously. Redinha they burned.

Wednesday, 13th. The enemy had marched all night, and we saw nothing of them till we came within two miles of Condeixa, where we found their army. Whilst our troops were bringing up, they marched off by the road to Miranda do Corvo, having first burned Condeixa.

Thursday, 14th. This was a day of incessant fighting; our advanced guard had not moved half a mile when the skirmishing began, and it continued for 2 leagues, until we came upon the entire of their army; as usual, whilst our troops were coming up they moved off.

Friday, 15th. A thick fog till 10 o'clock gave the enemy 4 hours start of us, and it was the evening before we came up with them; they were then discovered posted about the Alva. By a very brisk and skilful attack they were driven from some ground they held on this side the Alva, but it became dark before it could be ascertained whether they were all driven across the river.

Saturday Morning, 16th. The enemy is now posted close to the Alva, and I think it probable His Lordship will attack them there. Massena has ordered every town and village to be burned as they quit it, and too faithfully is the order obeyed—scarcely a house escapes. We take very few prisoners, their retreat being conducted in the most skilful manner; and was not Massena such a horrid monster of cruelty, I would praise his military skill. His Lordship, on his part, has shown himself an able General.

P.S.—Since I closed this, I have been to the advanced posts and find that the enemy is filing off without any apparent intention of making a stand at the Murcella position. They have their rear-guard strongly posted above the bridge which they have destroyed over the Alva. We have therefore come to a halt for the day, as we cannot repair the bridge whilst their rear-guard remains.

On March 29th, 1811, Jones set out from Lisbon to rejoin the army. "ALCOBACA, *April 3rd*—reached this place, once so exceedingly beautiful; lodged ourselves in the remains of an elegant house appertaining to the factory, which, with the whole town, and the venerable Convent is reduced to ashes by a party of French sent for the express purpose, and who left in the stables, that are alone undestroyed, green fodder that sufficed for our horses.

April 4. Before we left Alcobaca this morning, Ross and myself visited the Chapel, etc., found one solitary monk repairing the Royal

Tombs that had all been opened and broken. The body of Inez de Castro being exposed. The Library and Archives are preserved in an extraordinary manner, fire having evidently been lighted to consume them, etc. Sick and disgusted at scenes so depraved, and degrading to human nature, we went to Batalha,* which, being nearer the Great Road taken by the enemy has suffered considerably more than Alcobaca. Not a room in the Convent is left standing. The embalmed body of King John ('The Great'—the Founder of the Abbey, who, with his English wife, Philippa of Lancaster, had reposed here undisturbed, in a superb Mausoleum, for the space of four centuries) lay on the pavement in the middle of the Church; the bones scattered and mixed with others, designedly; and the Tombs rifled and defaced in the most wanton manner. Here, and at Alcobaca, all the organs were burnt to cinders."

To this brief account of malicious vandalism might be appended the narratives of other British officers—many of whom—like the author of the Diary, had often, on previous occasions, partaken of the generous and kindly hospitality of the monks of these two magnificent Convents.

Passing on, they—"found Leyria destroyed so much that we could with difficulty procure a quarter for the night." And thence to Condeixa—"formerly so famed for the beauty of its situation, etc.; with surprise and grief, found it burnt to the ground; not even a single house remaining; except those detached at a little distance in the valley below, where we took possession of a large house uninhabited."

All this was familiar ground, having been occupied by the British Army less than a year previously. The two officers now branched off the line of retreat, reaching Villa Pouca, April 7th—"where we were hospitably entertained by the principal proprietor, a well-informed old man who retained the country manners most completely." Thence onwards, they—"saw with regret the ruins of the large house at Cea, as well as many others we remembered." April 12th, they rejoined Head Qrs., meeting there Col. Fletcher and several other brother-officers.

Villa Formosa, April 14, 1811.

My Dear Father,

 . . . . I was obliged to remain at Lisbon to receive and distribute the Detacht. of Officers and men from England, there being no officer of our Corps in that city, and have consequently missed all the affairs our army have been engaged in during Massena's retreat. The Newspapers will

---

* For a detailed description of this noble building, the reader is referred to the sumptuous work of James Murphy:—*Plans, Elevations, and Views of the Royal Monastery of Batalha* (published in 1793). For the completion of this work, the author, who was an architect, resided for three months in the Monastery.

give you much better accounts of them than I can ; they have invariably been successful and brilliant ; but it is a question whether we have made the most of the opportunities so often afforded us of completing their rout and disorder. They are now however clear off to Ciudad Rodrigo and Salamanca, having left a garrison in Almeida, which fortress is completely surrounded by our troops ; but I believe we are not to commence any active operations against them, but content ourselves with merely blockading the place.

I was not able to settle everything and quit Lisbon until the 30th ; from that day to the 12th of the month I have been endeavouring to rejoin Head Qrs., and at length, after a march of nearly 300 miles through the country exhausted by the hostile armies, the towns and villages burnt, and the roads hardly passable, I have once more found them at this little village, about half a mile from the Spanish frontier, and 1½ or 2 leagues South of Almeida. I never experienced so many difficulties to impede one's progress as in this march ; only once or twice was I able to get any corn for my horses—never either hay or straw, and seldom any grass. My large horse was so very ill (in fact quite done up) that I was obliged to leave him behind me at Lisbon ; and my baggage pony being perfectly unable to get over the vile roads, with little or no food, I was obliged to exchange him on the road for a stronger baggage animal, giving an exorbitant price with him. It rained every day but the two last ; and notwithstanding all my purchases on the way, I had some trouble to get up with the army. To complete the business I am now ordered to join the troops in the Alemtejo, under Marshal Beresford, at Elvas or its vicinity, Lord Wellington having it in contemplation to besiege Badajoz has ordered all our officers that can be spared from other services, together with every requisite store for a siege, to be sent immediately to Elvas. Ross and 11 or 12 other officers are on their way there, and I shall set off the moment my stud is able to proceed. We do not as yet know whether Col. Fletcher will be allowed to go there himself, or indeed whether Lord Wellington may not take a trip in that direction ; should they not, Capt. Squire will be the senior, and have charge of the siege. For my own part I am not quite clear that it will ever be undertaken, and indeed I shall not be surprised if when we arrive at Elvas, and everything is ready, that we were all to be ordered back again. It is as yet a secret in the army.

Your very affectionate son,

RICE JONES.

"*April* 15. Set out for the Alemtejo this morning ; Lord Wellington taking with him none of his baggage, and but few attendants. Passed thro. Frenada, etc., to this town (Sabugal) which is nearly in the same ruinous state the French left it in, when they were driven out above a month since."

Next day's march to Pedrogoa Grande was—"principally over mountains covered with odoriferous shrubs ; the day very fine, and everything freshened by last night's rain ;—through Penamacor, an ancient fortress upon the steep slopes of a mountain. This is a good-sized village, little the worse for the French."   At Castello Branco, the next halting place "Lord Wellington occupied the Bishop's Palace."   And so on, through Nisa, to Portalegre, where the Qrs. "were very good and provisions plentiful ; the situation and scenery very fine," to Elvas, where Head Qrs. were established while Lord Wellington arranged with Marshal Beresford the course of future operations.

Matters had not been going well in the south of Portugal where Beresford was in command ; hence, says Napier, "The presence of the general-in-chief was agreeable to the troops ; they had seen great masses put in motion without any adequate results."   Wellington's instructions to Beresford had been to throw a bridge over the Guadiana at Jerumenha, push back the French under Mortier, and invest Olivenca and Badajoz.   Beresford, however,—" preferred halting for the means to cross at Jerumenha, and thus commenced in error those bloody operations which marred Wellington's great conceptions for carrying the war into Spain, and detained the army more than a year on the frontiers of Portugal."

Olivenca had surrendered on the 15th April—the day on which Wellington had set out for the Alemtejo ; but the governor of Badajoz had been allowed to repair the works and bring in materials and stores, unchecked.

CHAPTER EIGHT

Reverting to the Diary :—*April 21, 1811.* Lord Wellington and Col. Fletcher reconnoitred Badajoz.

April 24. Lord Wellington went back to Almeida. The Guadiana rose this night 7 ft. perpendicular, and carried away the bridge of boats at Jerumenha.

NOTE.—Napier tells us that, on the 24th, Wellington had forded the Guadiana, and pushing close up to Badajoz with a force of cavalry and infantry, endeavoured to cut off a convoy going to the place ; but the alert governor sallied, and the allies lost a hundred men without stopping the convoy.

Lord Wellington's sudden departure for the north again, was brought about by unexpected news that Massena was once more in motion. Meanwhile, preparations for the Siege of Badajoz were pushed forward. The Diary records the restoration of the bridge over the Guadiana on the 29th April ; the preparation of platforms, in the Arsenal at Elvas ; the Artificers being practised at Sapping ; and every exertion being made to procure cars.

The following observations by Napier with reference to the approaching siege are here quoted, as especially worthy of attention :—
" This was the first serious siege undertaken by the British in the Peninsula, and to the discredit of the English Government, no army was ever worse provided for such an enterprise. Without a corps of sappers and miners, they were compelled to attack fortresses defended by the most warlike, practised, and scientific troops of the age ; and the best officers and the finest soldiers sacrificed themselves in a lamentable manner to compensate for the negligence and incapacity of government. The sieges carried on by the British in Spain were a succession of butcheries, because the commonest materials and means necessary for their work were denied to the engineers."

We will now return to the Diary, observing that the author acted as Adjutant of Engineers during the siege :—

Elvas, May 4, 1811. Extremely hot weather. Maj.-Gen. Hon. W. Stewart invested Badajoz on the other side of the Guadiana this morning, with 3 Brigades of Infantry and a few Portuguese cavalry. Col. Fletcher and Jones went to meet Gen. Stewart, but returned in

the evening.   The 3 large boats moved to the situation chosen, near
the confluence of the Caya and Guardiana.

May 5.   The enemy reconnoitred very near our new bridge ; Col.
Fletcher, in consequence procured a battalion of the 17th Portuguese
Regt. for its protection.

7th.   Col. Fletcher moved to the camp before Badajoz.   Capt.
Squire and 2nd and 5th Brigades of Engineers left here to carry on the
attack against Ft. Christoval.   Lt. Forster reconnoitred to the foot of
the old Castle wall.

Elvas, May 7, 1811.

My Dear Father,

.   .   .   For my own part I never felt better in my life.   Lord
Wellington made a sudden move the day after I wrote to you from Villa
Formosa, and Col. Fletcher, and B.-Major Jones and myself came here at
the same time.   His Lordship remained here a few days only, during
which he reconnoitred Badajos, and determined upon undertaking the
siege, and then returned towards Almeida, leaving us here to carry it on.
Badajos was invested on the sides, on the left of the river Guadiana on the
4th Inst. but by some means (to us unaccountable) not a man have we
between this town and Badajos, or on the right bank of the river.   If the
investment is completed to-night, as I fully expect it will, we shall in all
probability break ground to-morrow night.   Col. Fletcher went from
hence to our camp before Badajos this morning ; I have some of his
arrangements to see executed, and rejoin him in the course of to-morrow.

It is now very late, you must therefore excuse the brevity of this epistle.

.   .   .   We have 21 officers of the Engineers here altogether.   I am
quite delighted at the prospect of witnessing the operations of a siege
such as this is likely to be.   .   .   .

Your very loving son,
Rice Jones.

8th.   Maj.-Gen. Lumley appeared before Ft. Christoval about 8
o'clock and completed the investment of Badajoz, with the loss of near
200 mên.   Capt. Squire broke ground this night before Ft. Christoval,
at 450 yds. ; the soil proved rocky, and the enemy opened a heavy
fire as soon as they began.   The 1st Brigade broke ground before the
Picourinho with 800 men ; and the 3rd on a false attack against Ft.
Pardilleros.

May 9th.   Having sent all our stores from Elvas, I moved to the
depôt before Badajoz ; found our Brig.-Maj. had arranged everything
for breaking ground before the body of the place at night.   At 5 p.m.,
Col. Fletcher returned to the depôt (having been all day with Sir W.
Beresford on the other side of the river) and countermanded all the
arrangements ; the Marshal having forbidden our proceeding this
night.   The party at work before St. Christoval were employed
during the day in raising the Battery and obtaining cover for the
guards.   The enemy kept up a heavy fire of guns, mortars and
musketry upon them, and their casualties were great.   Capt. Ross

and Boteler and Lt. Melville were wounded. The attacks against the Padrillera and Picourinho continued, and the enemy fired upon them occasionally, but without effect. At night the parties were employed in completing the batteries and parallels against the Picourinho and Padrillera. Capt. Squire's Brigades continued their work against St. Christoval, yet raised the battery but little from the extreme hardness of the soil, and the interruption given by the fire of the enemy.

Friday, May 10. The battery against the Picourinho completed and the guns mounted before 9 o'clock this morning. The parties continued raising the battery against St. Christoval. About 7 a.m., the enemy made a sortie with not less than 1,000 men and gained possession of the work for about a minute or two ; when they were driven back by the covering party. Lt. Reid, the engineer on duty, was slightly wounded, and distinguished himself by rallying the troops. Nominal reliefs sent to the false attack and that on the Picourinho ; the enemy fired occasionally, but did no harm on this side, but against the St. Christoval attack it was very heavy. Marshal Beresford still forbidding our proceeding with the attack against the body of the place, 200 yds. more of the parallel against the Picourinho was opened, and an approach of 250 yds. against the Padrillera was traced out and opened this evening in order to amuse the enemy on this side. The Battery against San Christoval was completed and the guns mounted, notwithstanding the heavy fire upon it. A Battery of 4 guns to enfilade the Bridge and prevent sorties, commenced this evening. Lt. Melville was killed by a cannon shot in the Battery against San Christoval at sunset. Marshal Beresford having given permission to commence operations against the place to-morrow evening, several car loads of stores were removed to the depôt near the Talavera road, during the night.

May 11. Soon after 2 a.m., set out to mark the directions of the intended attack, but was prevented in this by a thick fog at daylight ; small parties were employed at the false attack, and at the attack against the Picourinho ; the enemy showed some jealousy at the former and opened a fire upon it, but without effect. On the other side, the Battery to enfilade the bridge was much advanced. His country and the service sustained a severe loss in Capt. Dickinson whose head was carried off by a cannon shot, whilst standing on the parapet encouraging the workmen ; in him I have lost a sincere and valued friend and brother-officer. He was interred with Melville in Capella de Carvalho.

The Battery against San Christoval opened at daylight this morning ; the Portuguese Artillery directing the fire were inexperienced, and made very bad practice ; whilst the enemy kept up a very hot fire, and completely silenced it before night. The guns were withdrawn and the embrasures masked in the night ; another work was

begun this evening against the enemy's battery in the castle, under
cover of the hill, and on the left of that against San Christoval. The
Battery against the Picourinha fired nearly 200 rounds this day, but
produced not the smallest effect. 1,400 men were ordered to parade
at 6 o'clock, the tools arranged at the new depôt, and everything was
ready to commence our attack at the body of the place, when at
5 p.m., Col. Fletcher received notice of the arrival of our stores at
Elvas, the Portuguese tools being very bad, and it being of consequence to secure sufficient cover before daylight, it was judged
expedient to defer the attack until next night, and a letter was sent
to Marshal Beresford acquainting him with this determination. At
7 p.m., an order was received from the Marshal to suspend the work
and the conveyance of stores across the river, for the present ; orders
were therefore sent to stop the stores from Lisbon, which Capt. By,
and afterwards myself, were sent to Elvas to hurry on. I slept at
Elvas this night.

Sunday, May 12. Returned from Elvas this morning. At one
o'clock Sir W. Beresford consented to our breaking ground this night.
The tools which had been sent back by the Marshal's order of last
evening were immediately ordered up again ; but it was $\frac{1}{2}$ past 7
before they could be got to the ground where the working party (1,400
men) and the covering party (1,500) were paraded ; and it was
between 8 and 9 before they could be distributed. The weather
which had hitherto been extremely fine became suddenly cloudy this
afternoon, with rain, and the night was uncommonly dark and cloudy
until 10 o'clock, when the moon rose and the weather became clear.
The party were immediately set to work, and opened a parallel 800
yds. in length, at 600 yds. from the place, and an approach 600
yds. to the rear. The soil proved so very favourable and the men
worked so well, being unperceived by the enemy, that the parallel
was generally 3 ft., and 3 ft. 6 in. deep, by 4 ft. in width, and there
was every prospect of being well covered before daylight, when, at
1 a.m. on the morning of the 13th, orders were received to withdraw
the workmen from the trenches, and send the stores to the rear.
The working and covering parties were then withdrawn, unperceived
by the enemy, and all our means of transport employed to convey our
stores over the Guadiana. Parties were employed during the night
on the batteries against San Christoval ; when the moon rose the
enemy opened a fire upon the new lower battery.

May 13. All our cars employed in carrying away stores to the
right bank of the Guadiana ; the stores not worth carriage, or for
which carriage could not be procured were ordered to be destroyed.
Sent with this order to Capt. Squire at the camp before San Christoval ; visited the batteries against that fort and returned by the ford
near our new depôt. A pile of timber, fascines, and gabions were
burnt there this night.

May 14. At 6 a.m., Col. Fletcher ordered some of the stores crossing the Guadiana to be detained, and officers were sent in every direction to counter order the march of the stores to Elvas, in consequence of a communication from Sir W. Beresford of his uncertainty respecting the advance of the enemy. Shortly after, Capt. Rovena came and informed the Col. that General Cole had received an order to move the two Divisions of his army and raise the investment of the place. I was therefore sent to countermand the orders just given, and went on to Elvas to give the like directions to Mr. Davis. All our stores were over the river this evening. As soon as it became dark all our batteries were dismantled, and the platforms taken up and sent to the right bank of the river.

May 15. Showery weather. The flying bridge taken up and sent to Jurumenha, as were the officers and the artificers. The Marshal wrote to Col. Fletcher recommending him to secure the passages across the Guadiana during this rainy weather, as the ultimate safety of his army might depend upon it. The Col. in consequence, went to inspect them himself, and went this evening to Jurumenha, on his way to join the army. The enemy felt our pickets this morning to learn if the army had withdrawn from before the place, and succeeded in killing and wounding about 90 of our men in the evening. General Cole withdrew his Division at midnight, and finally raised the investment of the place ; General Lumley having previously marched from before San Christoval. Attended Col. Fletcher to Jurumenha ; arrived there after dark.

CAMP BEFORE BADAJOS, May 15, 1811.

MY DEAR FATHER,

A mail leaves this for England to-night, and though I have hardly a moment to spare, I cannot let it go without informing you of the disgraceful termination of our attack upon Badajos, and of my continued health and safety. The investment having been completed on the morning of the 8th Inst. batteries were that night commenced against Fort San Christoval, on the right bank of the river, opposite the town, and against two outworks on the south side . . . those upon the two latter being merely intended as a feint to draw the attention of the besieged to that side, whilst the real attack was to be upon the walls of an old castle which encloses Badajos on the north side, and have not the advantage of being covered by a ditch or covert way. Marshal Beresford was pressed to allow us to begin this our principal attack on the next night, (the 9th) in order that Marshal Soult might not be able to interrupt us before the fall of the place, and which the Colonel (Fletcher) calculated would take place in five days from the time we opened our first parallel; but it was not until the night of the 12th that the Marshal finally consented to our beginning; we however broke ground that night at between 5 and 600 yards from the walls, and had obtained tolerable good cover the whole length of our parallel (800 yards), when, at one o'clock on the morning of the 13th, an order arrived to stop everything, and during that day and yesterday all our artillery and stores were removed back into Elvas; nothing could have been going on better than we were when this order was received—occasioned, it is said, by a report of Marshal Soult being on his march towards this place. Marshal Beresford with his army (excepting a Division left to watch the Fortress, and they, I believe, will retire in the night) have marched; his Head Qrs. were to-day at Valverde, 4 leagues off.

. . . .

The attack upon Fort Christoval was continued all this time in the most determined manner by Capt. Squire. . . . The enemy also conducted their defence with great skill and spirit, and on the morning of the 10th made a sortie in considerable numbers, and succeeded in getting possession of our battery, but were speedily driven out of it again. . . . The officers of our Corps have suffered much; my worthy friend, Capt. Dickenson, and Lieut. Melville fell in the batteries. . . . I have not patience to write more on such a melancholy subject; hoping that justice awaits those who are guilty of all our loss and disgrace,

I remain yours,

RICE JONES.

P.S.—We go to-day to Marshal Beresford's Head Qrs., and if nothing goes on, shall, I imagine, return to Lord Wellington's army shortly.

NOTE.—For the better understanding of the recent operations, it is necessary to turn to Napier's remarks thereon :—

"At this time (May 11th) five engineers had fallen and 700 officers and soldiers of the line had been inscribed upon the bloody list of victims offered to this Moloch, and only one small battery against an outwork was completed. On the 11th it opened, and before sunset the fire of the enemy had disabled 4 of its 5 guns, and killed many more of the besiegers; nor could any other result be expected, because the concert essential to success in double operations, whether in sieges or the field was totally neglected by Beresford. Then, having received intelligence that the French Army was in movement, he arrested the progress of all the works. On the 12th, believing this information premature, he directed the trenches to be opened against the castle; yet the intelligence was true, and being confirmed at 12 o'clock at night, measures were taken to raise the siege."

The fact is, Soult had resolved to succour Badajoz. On the 14th he reached Villa Franca, and being then within 30 miles of Badajoz, fired salvoes during the night, to give notice of his approach to the garrison. Meanwhile, Beresford, after a conference with the Spanish generals, determined to meet the attack of the French Army at Albuera, which battle was fought the day after the siege was raised; viz., May 16.

Resuming the Diary :—

May 16. The morning was far advanced before Col. Fletcher and I left Jurumenha; passing near Olivenca, we heard of the action this morning; rode as hard as we could towards the scene; before we reached Valverde met a good many servants, Baggage, etc., going to the rear ; as we approached the Field, some of the wounded, amongst others, General Cole. Joined Marshal Beresford and remained with the staff. Towards evening the Marshal and suite went into the village of Albuera, intending to dine there on what could be procured, but obliged to evacuate ; though the Germans under General Alten did not give up possession of it. The enemy having the bridge could force them out when they liked. Lay on the field near the 34th Regt. Major Dickens affording us all the aid he could ; rainy and uncomfortable all night ; the ground being so very wet, and no shelter to be found.

May 17. Both armies occupied, all this day, the same ground as yesterday afternoon. During the night we slept under arms as before, but got a little refreshment from Col. Dickson.

May 18. At daybreak it appeared the enemy moved off last night. Rode on with the Spanish cavalry, in pursuit of them, until we came upon a body of their cavalry consisting of 25 Squadrons ; when the Spaniards halted and the Conde de Penha Villamor sent me to inform Marshal Beresford whom I soon after met. Col. Fletcher, Jones and myself came here (Olivenca) upon our way back to Elvas, and procured good Qrs.

Elvas, Sunday, 19. Upon our arrival, found Lord Wellington just arrived from Almeida.

NOTE.—Napier tells us that Lord Wellington, after examining the state of affairs, directed the 3rd and 7th Divisions to complete the reinvestment of Badajoz on the right bank, and directed the renewed Siege of Badajoz in person. Resuming the Diary :—

Camp before Badajoz, May 29, 1811. Left Elvas about noon, after making all the necessary arrangements for the siege ; found the stores in Depôt, and the troops bivouacing round Badajoz. *May* 30*th*. 300 men were employed last night at the false attack upon fort Pardeleras, and continued at it all this day. *May* 31. Soon after it became dusk last night, the parallel from the Talavera road, for 1,100 yds. towards the river, and the approach from the Parks began to be opened ; two parties of 400 men each employed upon the former, and the same number upon the latter, which was about 1,000 yds. in length. The covering party consisted of 1,200, disposed in two large bodies before the centre of the parallel, with strong detachments upon each flank, and pickets and single Light Infantry pushed out in front. The enemy failed to discover the work before morning, when they opened a fire of six guns. At the San Christoval attack four batteries were commenced :—No. 1 of 5 guns against the Castle ; No. 2 of 3 guns and 2 howitzers to breach the exposed flank of Fort San Christoval at 400 yds. dist. ; No. 3 a battery of 4 guns to destroy the interior defences of the fort at 800 yds. dist. ; No. 4 for 4 guns and 2 howitzers used as mortars, to enfilade the bridge and intercept the communications between the Fort and the Town. A parallel was also begun connecting the batteries; the working party employed consisted of 1,200 men; the covering party of 800. The enemy discovered their party and kept up a fire during the whole night.

NOTE.—From May 31st to the night of June 2nd the Diary gives full details of the number of men employed, and of the nature of their work. By the evening of June 2, " The batteries were all armed and furnished with ammunition."

June 3. At ½ past 9 this morning the batteries all opened; fired very inaccurately all day; but brought the old wall of the castle down before evening.

NOTE.—Full details of the siege works being given by Napier—and in greater detail by Sir John Jones, I pass on to the entry for June 6th :—*June 6th* to *7th*. At midnight the breach in the Flank of Fort San Christoval was assaulted without success. The advance of 25 men was led by Lieut. Forster who was mortally wounded at the close of the fight, which continued for more than an hour, with the greatest obstinacy on both sides. The foot of the breach said to have been cleared by the enemy to the height of 7 feet after it became dark in the evening.

After this failure, more guns were mounted, the fire resumed, and preparations completed for a renewed assault.

Sunday, June 9. At the end of this day's firing the rubbish in the castle breach was considerably increased; and the breach in the flank of San Christoval is again said to be practicable. At 9 this evening the party moved out of the works to assault Fort San Christoval, led by Lt. Hunt, who was killed on the glacis. The enemy being prepared gave them a sharp reception; the party consisting of 200, with an advance of 25, got into the ditch, where the Comdg. officer was killed. The attack continued about an hour, when the remains of the party, unable to force the breach, were recalled. The quantity of shells and combustibles thrown by the enemy into the ditch was enormous. We lost forty killed and 100 wounded.

June 10. At ten o'clock this morning a truce was obtained to bury our dead, during which I advanced to the French Picquet on the Rivellas to ascertain the fate of a Portuguese serjeant who was shot whilst accompanying me in reconnoitring the breach last night. In consequence of the movements of Marshals Soult and Marmont, and the deplorable state of our artillery, Lord Wellington, after the failure of last night's assault, determined to raise the siege.

June 12. The siege finally raised; the guns and stores being all retired. Our losses in the operations of the siege were 9 officers and 109 men killed and 25 officers and 350 men wounded and missing. *June* 19. The French armies under Soult and Marmont having joined, entered Badajoz.

Camp before Badajos, *June* 12, 1811.

My dear Father,

My last letter dated the 15th of May informed you of the chagrin we all felt at being obliged to raise the siege of Badajos ; my present, I am sorry to say, has the like unfortunate news to communicate. After 12 days of open trenches, and 8 days battering, we have a second time sent our artillery and stores across the Guadiana to Elvas, and are now about to break up, and remove to that place ourselves. I have not time to send you a detail of our daily operations, and indeed it would be of but little use, as the newspapers will give it at greater length. However, I will just run over the dates of events as they happened since my last. The afternoon of that day we went from the camp to Jurumenha, for the purpose of inspecting the bridges across the Guadiana at that place, upon the security of which the safety of our army would entirely depend in the event of its meeting with a defeat. The next morning I proceeded with Col. Fletcher to join Marshal Beresford ; upon the road we heard that his army was then engaged with that of Marshal Soult, and we of course pushed our horses to their utmost to get up in time ; but before we could reach the field, the enemy were repulsed, and were quietly reposing on their own ground. I thus unfortunately missed the sanguinary battle of Albuera. We remained upon the ground that night, as well as the whole of the 17th in expectation of another attack ; the whole French army being drawn out in front of us. During that night they began to retire, and the morning of the 18th found only their cavalry before us, which soon moved in compact order, being not less than 20 Squadrons, upon their principal routes. We then returned to Elvas on the 19th, and met Lord Wellington who with the 3rd and 7th Divisions had marched from Almeida after their repulse of Massena near that place. His Lordship immediately decided upon undertaking the siege of Badajos again, and upon the 29th of May we opened ground before Fort Paderillas, as a feint to draw the attention of the enemy to that quarter ; the next night we began our approaches and parallel on the low ground before the old castle that I described to you before. . . . On the 10th it was determined to raise the siege, the reinforcements for Soult being at hand, and the old walls having proved so very hard and tough as to baffle all calculations as to the time when a practicable breach could be effected with the old, miserable Portuguese guns, which were nearly all disabled by our firing ; and, added to our having expended nearly the whole of the shot and shells from Elvas, were I imagine the motives of this decision of his Lordship's.

We lost two very fine young men, Lts. Forster and Hunt, leading the storming parties to the assault ; Capt. Patton was severely wounded, but I trust is doing well, and Capt. Mulcaster lies extremely ill from a fever brought on by excessive fatigue. I have met with several narrow escapes in common with the others, and have much reason to be thankful for having gone with safety through both sieges. . . .

Your very loving son,

Rice Jones.

Note.—Here again failure was due to the inadequacy and inferior quality of the means available. The guns,—says Sir J. Jones, were of brass, false in their bore, and already worn by previous service ; and the shots were of all shapes and diameters, giving a windage from 1-10th to half an inch. The chambers of the howitzers used as mortars were all of unequal size, the shells did not fit the bore, and their beds were unsteady, so that the practice was vague and uncertain. The very tools,—says Napier, were unfit for work ; the French cutting instruments were eagerly sought for in preference ;—"and when the soldiers' lives, and the honour of England were at stake, English cutlery would not bear comparison with French !"

Sir John Jones, in his review of the operations, thus sums up :—" The most critical examination of the operations of this siege will not allow of blame for its failure being thrown on any one. From the general to the soldier each did his duty ; nor should the want of success discredit the original project. It must be admitted that there was a judicious application of all the means that could be collected for the reduction of Christoval. On trial those means proved insufficient ; many of the causes of their insufficiency could not have been foreseen, and others, if foreseen, could not have been remedied ; all that skill and bravery could effect was done."

Lord Wellington, in one of his Despatches, wrote, "I believe the failure in the attack upon San Christoval is, like many other events, to be attributed to the want of experience in the British army."

Napier, writing many years afterwards, with complete knowledge of the circumstances, and with due deliberation, declared that, "Fifteen days of open trenches and nine days of fire was all that could be expected, and with good guns, plentiful stores, and a corps of regular sappers and miners this time would have sufficed ; but none of these things were in camp, and it was a keen jest of Picton's, that 'Lord Wellington sued Badajos *in forma pauperis.*'"

Sir John T. Jones, in his "Journal of the Sieges," also remarked on the inefficiency of the Portuguese artillerymen, who "though brave and zealous, were very young and inexperienced, and after a few rounds their practice became very uncertain." And yet strange to say, in recording the siege operations at Olivença, a few weeks earlier, and which resulted in the capture of that fortress, and in which these same "young and inexperienced" Portuguese gunners worked the breaching batteries, the same writer tells us that "the artillery consisted of a company of Portuguese artillery under Capt. Jose de San Payo," and that, although "composed principally of young soldiers, showed a good deal of spirit and steadiness ; for though exposed to a brisk fire and a good deal of musketry, which killed two and wounded six others in the breaching battery, scarcely a shot was thrown away." In comparing Sir John Jones' account of the Siege of Badajoz, with the entries in Rice Jones' Diary, there is a curious similarity, which seems to suggest that the distinguished author of the " Journal of Sieges " drew extensively on his friend's " Diary " for the narrative.

Some idea of the inferior material with which this siege had been undertaken may be gathered from the Diary of Sir Alex. Dickson, who, as a Capt. of artillery was in charge of that branch at the siege ; he wrote,—" The guns we got from Elvas for the siege of Badajoz were brass Portuguese guns of the time of John IV. and his son Affonso, bearing the dates 1646, 1652. Also some Spanish guns of 1620." The comment of Sir J. Jones on the operations is to the following effect :—" Everything else was on the same scale of inferiority, and it may be considered as fortunate that the approach of Marshal Soult's army caused the siege to be raised ; as otherwise, after a further sacrifice of men in other feeble attempts, it would have brought itself to a conclusion from inability to proceed."

From June 22nd onwards, Jones was at Campo Major,—" assisting Capt. McCleod in the erection of a line of sham works towards Ougella, an old castle, occupied by a few Portuguese." Early in July, he joined the Light Division,—" bivouacing in the woods, where we continued quiet until the 23rd ; when Head Qrs. removed to Porta-legre, and the Light Division occupied Castello and the adjacent villages ; but I was not well enough to accompany it, and remained at Elvas until the end of the month. *August 3.* Rejoined General Craufurd at Bemposta."

(Undated—probably July).

My dear Father,

There is nothing new to inform you since my last. I am now with the Light Division on the Caya, about 3 leagues above Elvas ; the rest of the army are on the same river or in its vicinity, between Arronches and Elvas, and Head Qrs. are still at San Vincente. We have heard nothing certain of the enemy's movements lately. General Craufurd has thus far behaved civilly enough ; and Ross and his troop of Horse Artillery, who are attached to the Division, are particularly kind. . . .

P.S.—Since writing this I find that 2 Divisions marched this morning towards Castello Branco, and it is said the others will follow.

NOTE.—The Light Division resumed its march on August 7th passing a village very beautifully situated in a " wood of beautiful Chestnut trees, and near a very fine stream of running water ; " and bivouacking for the night in a wood of fine large chestnut trees. Thence onwards, till, on the 9th Fuente Guinaldo—just inside the Spanish frontier—is reached—" a good town ; the best we have seen since we quitted the Alemtejo." Next morning the march was resumed before daylight, and Mortiago reached the same evening, in heavy rain.

From Capt. S. R. Chapman.

PALL MALL, *Aug.* 6, 1811.

DEAR JONES,

. . . I think it likely you will soon be ordered home, to take possession of your appointment to one of the Adjutancies ; I suppose in the first instance you will go to Woolwich. . . . As your new appointment is of a permanent character, at any rate it is so till further promotion . . . I hope you feel more comfortable with an Epaulette, tho' with a Frinze ; the rank you have obtained is I think one of the most important steps in our Corps. . . .

The R.M. Artificers, which I hope will soon be called Royal Sappers and Miners, are to be taught to construct Batteries, Trenches, etc., etc., and I hope with the care that is to be taken to instruct them properly, they will be found to be a very useful body of men. . . .

Yours ever sincerely,

S. R. CHAPMAN.

Addressed to :—

CAPT. RICE JONES,
    Royal Engineers,
        British Army, Portugal, Lt. Division.

Aug. 11. Marched at daylight ; lay upon our arms at Zamarra for some time, until Genl. Murray came and ordered us to march towards Ciudad Rodrigo. At the ruined Convent of Caridade met some squadrons of Dragoons, and Cpt. Bull's troop of Horse Artly. Left the Division near the ford by the Convent, and went with General Craufurd to reconnoitre the place, taking 20 of the Royal Dragoons as our escort. Rode round at the distance of 1,000 to 1,800 yds. from the works, to the height in front of San Francisco. The new work constructed by the French appears small ; the ditch seems respectable, and the work well manned. New embrasures are making in the principal enceinte of the place, particularly in the faces fronting the suburb on the Salamanca Road. In the afternoon we returned to Martiago by the same road, a good deal fatigued from the heat of the day, and the roughness of the roads.

NOTE.—In explanation of the above, it may be stated that Wellington, so Napier writes, learning from an intercepted despatch that Ciudad Rodrigo was in want of provisions, and hoping to profit from this circumstance, crossed the Tagus at Villa Velha early in August, and moved by Castello Branco towards that fortress, pretending he sought healthy cantonments. He had already planned to take Rodrigo by surprise ; for which purpose he had caused a battering train just arrived from England with their gunners to be secretly landed at Oporto, carried up the Douro in boats to Lamego, whence they were taken to Villaponte near Celorico, without attracting attention. " The bringing of 68 huge guns, with proportionate stores across fifty miles of mountain was an operation of magnitude ; 5,000 draft

bullocks were required for the train alone, and above 1,000 militia
were, for several weeks, employed merely to repair the road ; the
effort,"—adds Napier, " marred one of Napoleon's formidable
projects."

August 15. Hearing the French are making an incursion into the
Sierra, General Craufurd set out with an orderly Portuguese dragoon
and myself through Saugo to the Puerto, or pass above Gata—distant
4 leagues, the greater part footpath, through low brushwood, etc.
After some consideration we descended the pass on the South side
by a paved road for about a league to the town of Gata ; met a
Spaniard with a letter concealed in his clothes giving an account of
the visit of the enemy to the towns in the Sierra, and stating they
retired from Gata in the morning. Although Gata is an inviting
town, and the inhabitants appeared well-disposed, the General conceived it would be imprudent to sleep there, as the enemy's movements were unknown, and seemed uncertain. We therefore went a
league further to Cadalso ; upon our arrival found a French Proclamation just posted up in the Market-place ; but being too tired to
proceed, were obliged to stay at Cadalso ; from whence the next day
we returned by Escargo Maria and Robledilla to Martiago.

Martiago, August 14, 1811.

My dear Father,

Since my last letter we have made rather a long march, and instead of
being near Badajoz, we are now about 3 leagues from Ciudad Rodrigo.
A variety of reasons are assigned for this movement, but I am so utterly
ignorant on the subject that I will not venture to send any one of them.
Some say we are going to besiege Ciudad Rodrigo, but of this I must
confess I have some doubts. We arrived here on the 10th inst., the next
day we made a kind of reconnaisance of the place, and returned here in
the evening ; since when we have halted, and are cantoned in the neighbouring villages. Where the rest of the army are I cannot tell, but I
believe somewhere on this side of the Coa. Head Qrs. are at Fuente
Guinalda, 3 leagues west of this village. I am extremely comfortable
with this Division ; it is always in front, and if anything occurs is sure of
having its share. General Craufurd is particularly civil, and although
he rides hard every day, and knocks up my horses, which are not the
best in the world, yet he keeps one of the best tables in the army, and as
I live with him, and my health is such as to enable me to stand the
fatigue, I do very well.

I have not heard a word of the Adjutancy ;—indeed I would rather not
(whilst there is anything going on in this country) be ordered to return at
once. It is very odd that Major Chapman has not answered any of my
letters on the subject ; but I suppose he is very busy, or, else, like some
others, has learnt the importance attached to an official character, whether
in the Ordnance Office or the Inspector-General's.

I have not a word of news to write to you this time. . . .

Your very affectionate son,
Rice Jones.

Note.—The following letter, which appeared in the London *Times*, may well find a place here at this stage of the war :—

From The Times of 1811.

Thursday, August 29.

TO THE EDITOR OF THE TIMES

Sir,—As the public seem at present rather out of spirits respecting our progress in the Peninsula, and as the great influence which *The Times* possesses over the public sentiment has always been exerted in supporting the determination of the country to maintain its honour and existence, I submit to you a few ideas, which will, I am persuaded, give a material turn to the sentiments of our countrymen, who are too apt to be elated beyond reasonable bounds in the hour of success, and unnecessarily dejected, if the prospect appears even *momentarily* altered.

When Lord Wellington was following Massena to the frontiers of Portugal, Englishmen expected that the whole French army (150,000 men) were to be driven over the Pyrenees in six weeks. His Lordship is now on the defensive; and we begin to contemplate the probability of a return to Torres Vedras. Let it, however, be recollected, that Lord Wellington's movements, though not marked with the brilliant results of great victories—of captured cannon, of standards, or wounded prisoners,— have yet had the following *solid* effects :—

1st. *The recovery of the whole province of Asturias*, and the consequent advantages of recruiting the Spanish force by new levies—of posting those levies in almost inaccessible mountains—and of lessening the resources (of subsistence, etc.) of the enemy. 2dly. The recapture of Astorga, which cost the French a long siege, and near 2,000 men. 3dly. A loss to the foe of not less than 4 or 5,000 men, from desertion (see accounts from Corunna), sickness, and fatigue (*vide* Sanchez' action, etc.). 4thly. Immense fatigue to the French forces, who have marched several hundred miles, and have now to retrace their steps. And 5thly. The increase of the Spanish Guerilla force, which has received an accession of at least 4,000 men. Are not these results fully equal to any thing which even a splendid victory could have produced? And these results have been produced without our having to regret the loss of five or ten thousand brave men.

In a word, is the situation of the French improved since August, 1810? Are they nearer to the conquest of the Peninsula? In August, 1810, they had 200,000 men in the country—were acting on the offensive, and penetrating into Portugal. They have now about 136,000,—dare not look at Portugal,—have lost 10,000 square miles of the territory they held in Spain,—and are everywhere on the defensive ;—and so threatened and harassed, as to be obliged to run from one post to another to meet the threatened attack,—first rushing to the south, and then hastening back to the north : one moment assembling—again subdividing ; and daily losing men, ground, and *confidence*.

I am, etc.,

Norwich, Aug. 24.

R.M.

August 16. Bivouac near El Casar. Proceeded with Lieut. Scott, 95th Regt., to Robledilla and instructed him to post himself and his party of the 95th to guard the pass. Procured a guide from Robledilla, and went along the Eastern ridge of the valley running from Robledilla to Cadalso, for some distance; then took a turn to the left and descended into a cultivated country, and soon after reached Toricilla; stopt there but little, the enemy being in Villa Nueva, about 3 miles and within sight; proceeded to El Pino and from thence to Cavar de Paloma, where I met Capt. Grant who is employed to obtain intelligence, and was well known to all the people in the neighbourhood. After dining with him, rather scantily, we led our horses by some by-paths to a garden near a brook, where Grant thought we might sleep in security under the shelter of some Olive trees.

August 19. Breakfasted on Roasted Potatoes, and left Grant, proceeding by El Pino up a narrow valley never visited by French or English, and, from its situation, nearly inaccessible. Ascended by a long and dangerous path to the Puerto Vieja, from whence the descent is much easier to Martiago.

August 22. Accompanied Genl. Craufurd to Mayllo, through Moras Verdes, in order to make ourselves acquainted with the country. *Aug.* 23. From Mayllo we proceeded through Cuceado to Sequeros, a village finely situated near the right of a hill looking over Miranda de Castanar to Bijar; but troops of the enemy being close round us, and expected to arrive for their rations levied on the village, we remained only long enough to bait, and descended to Villa Nueva del Conde, a larger place, but not so pleasing; received with acclamations when known to be English; but passed through without stopping and proceeded by an intricate road through Valero and San Miguel de Valero, to Linhares, where we remained the night, and were well entertained by the Padrè Curé. Returned to Martiago next day, by a different route.

Martiago, August 28th, 1811.

My dear Father,

. . . The day before yesterday I received a letter from Major Chapman, wherein he tells me that upon General Morse's resignation he had not failed to speak to General Mann about my Adjutancy, though he did not believe that his former application would have been passed over, " besides which," says he, " Handfield is much your friend, and I think it likely you will soon be ordered home to take possession of your appointment; I suppose in the first instance you will go to Woolwich; let me know how you will like this." He likewise states his expectation of seeing the Ryl. Military Artificers called Ryl. Sappers and Miners very soon; and as they are to be drilled in the construction of batteries, trenches, saps, &c., trusts that they will prove a useful body of men; I hope they may, but I cannot say that my expectations are very sanguine on that head; altering their name is undoubtedly doing something, but

107

whilst they are kept constantly at work in the different shops at Woolwich, Chatham, or Portsmouth, and without officers who can be responsible for the companies wherever they may be, (which is at present the case)—for the Commdg. Engineers have neither the time or inclination to undertake the task, and the superannuated Sergt.-Majors, who were, 3 or 4 years ago made Sub. Lts. are totally incapable of it. If they will give me the charge of a Battalion, to be disciplined like other soldiers, and taught sapping, etc., so as to be useful in the field, I shall feel happy in devoting my time to the attainment of what will prove so highly useful to the service, and creditable to ourselves. But if the name only is to be changed, and the men, after working all the week, are to be drilled and become soldiers on Sundays, and the King's Birthday, only, I shall for ever regret my having returned from such a desirable and honourable service, to partake of the disgrace that such a set of undisciplined Vagabonds must bring upon anyone that has anything to do with them.

I enter thus largely upon this topic, that you may not be surprised if, upon my entering into the duties of my Adjutancy and finding it impossible to discharge those duties creditably, I should without hesitation prefer (as I undoubtedly ever will) to return to my duty as an officer of Engineers, wherever they may choose to send me. However, I now indulge somewhat of the hope of getting a respectable Battn. of Sappers ; and future armies will not, I trust, find themselves before another Badajos, without a single man who had seen, much less worked, at a *Sap*, which requires so much practice to carry on at all; whilst at the same time the French Corps of Sappers and Miners are the finest body of men in their army.

We remain here exactly the same as when I wrote to you last ; but the enemy have within these few days past evinced an intention of moving from Plascencia and Valladolid, so as to prevent our besieging Ciudad Rodrigo, for which purpose every preparation has been making ; although I do not believe that we can under present circumstances venture to take our battering train, etc., across the river Agueda ; and without which we cannot undertake the siege. A week or ten days will probably show us what they intend doing. I do not feel very confident that we can remain very long so far advanced into Spain as we are at this moment. I shall do all in my power to remain with Genl. Craufurd until things take a turn, either one way or the other. If the army advances we shall be in front ; and if it retires, our Division will form the Rear Guard. Added to this the civility and attention I constantly receive from the General, and you will, I am sure, agree with me, in conceiving it highly desirable that I should remain here whilst any active service is going on. They are not in general very quick at our office, and I therefore hope I may not receive my orders to return just yet.

Should I land at Falmouth or Plymouth, I will not fail to see you on my way to London, at least if you are at Bristol, or anywhere near the road ; but, as affairs now are, I think you had better continue writing to me here. . . .

Your very affectionate son,

RICE JONES.

CHAPTER NINE

NOTE.—The following sketch of Wellington's most trusted and daring Intelligence Officer, Capt. Colquhoun Grant, mentioned above, was published anonymously, some time ago :—

It is much to be regretted that the Duke of Wellington never condescended to write the history of his intercourse with Capt. Colquhoun Grant. A volume on that subject written by such an accurate and unimaginative chronicler as the Duke of Wellington would have been a classic for all time. On such a theme, the baldest and most prosaic recital of the hero's deeds would have been more thrilling than a novel. That he acted habitually under the guidance of the Duke of Wellington, and held communication with no other English officer, is well known ; but it was also his invariable practice to wear his uniform wherever he went and never to assume any disguise. Of course, his usual method of entering the enemy's lines was in the character of a deserter from the British army ; and the excuses which he invented to account for his desertion were as inexhaustible as they were ingenious. Sometimes he posed as a cavalry trooper, and sometimes as a private in an infantry regiment who had stolen a thoroughbred horse from some Staff officer on which to make his escape with salutary speed. He was generally attended by a Spanish peasant named Leon, upon whose quickness of apprehension, fidelity, and vigilance he placed, after some experience of his good qualities, the most absolute reliance.

Hanging on the flank of Marmont's army until it passed the Coa, the indomitable Colquhoun Grant soon discovered that the French had left their scaling-ladders behind them, and, therefore, had no real intention to attempt the recapture of Ciudad Rodrigo. Being anxious to ascertain by what route Marmont would proceed to Coimbra, whither his head was pointed, Colquhoun Grant and Leon (the latter on foot) hid themselves on a low ridge, covered with dwarf oaks, at the foot of which lay a pass which the French army seemed likely to traverse. Unfortunately, some French sharpshooters, posted on a higher ridge, descried the two companions as they withdrew from the road below and plunged into the forest. In a few minutes a cry of " The French ! the French ! " issued from Leon's lips, and the foe, represented by a dozen mounted dragoons, was upon them. Exhausted by running, poor Leon fell, and was instantly

"

transfixed and killed by a French spear. Striving in vain to protect his fallen friend, Grant was captured and carried before Marmont. The latter, who was one of the few gentlemen to be found among Napoleon's Marshals, treated his prisoner kindly and invited him to dinner. As usual, his uniform saved his life ; but after they had left Marmont's headquarters, under an escort charged to convey him from Spain to France, Grant found to his surprise, on arriving at Bayonne, that Marmont had written to the commandant of that town and garrison explaining that Grant was a very dangerous and daring spy, who had done the French armies in Spain no end of harm, and that he was to be put in irons and sent to Paris.

They had to reckon, however, with no ordinary man in Colquhoun Grant. Divining the contents of Marmont's letter, by that intuitive instinct which, like a cat's whiskers, guided him in the dark, he contrived to escape from Bayonne by night, scrambling down into a deep fosse upon his trusty thoroughbred, from whom he had never parted company, and climbing up the almost perpendicular slope on the other side. By some kind of freemasonry, known only to bold spirits, he introduced himself on the road to General Souham, who was on his way back to Paris, and craved permission to join his party. Describing himself under a false name as a paroled British officer, Grant delighted his companions with his versatility, and by his description of moving adventures which he invented for their amusement. On arriving in Paris, he made himself known to another English spy, who had long been a member of the French police, and in constant communication with English agents, who carried his secret reports verbally to London, which they reached through Spain, Antwerp, or Rotterdam. His Parisian colleague told him that a passport had just been made out in favour of Jonathan Buck, an American, who had died suddenly on the day when the passport ought to have been claimed. Boldly demanding this passport, which carried him safely through every obstruction, Grant rode his faithful steed down to Nantes, where he intended to embark on an American ship. Her departure was, however, delayed, and with his accustomed courage, he told the American captain his story, and sought his advice. With kindly sympathy the American skipper bade him assume the character of a discontented sailor, and supplying him with a rough nautical dress and with forty dollars, told him to lodge the money in the American Consul's hands, upon which he would receive a certificate authorising him as a discharged seaman to proceed from port to port in search of a ship.

August 30, 1811. Accompanied Genl. Craufurd by the left of the Pass of El Fortin. The Guerillas of Don Juan Sanchez dancing, etc., by moonlight with the inhabitants. *Sunday, Aug.* 31. Rode with the General along the ridge of the Sierra towards Torredecilla, till we could overlook Cadalso. Came back to Robledilla to dinner in the evening by way of the Convent of N, S. de los Angelos, where we were very hospitably treated. Returned next morning to Martiago.

NOTE.—From Sept. 1st onwards, Jones was employed daily in examining the country, either with Genl. Craufurd or alone, or riding over to Lord Wellington's Head Qrs. at Guinaldo, where, on Sept. 12, he found orders for him to return to England. (By Genl. Mann, dated Aug. 16).

Sept. 18. Genl. Craufurd went with Wood towards Tamanes, to ascertain the movements of the enemy, who show an evident intention to relieve Ciudad Rodrigo. Rode with Ross to Las Agallas, to the position where his guns are to be posted ; returned in the evening.

General Craufurd remained at the front till the 21st, when a body of the enemy's cavalry entering Tamanes obliged him to retire to Martiago again. *Sept.* 23. The Light Division took post along the Vadilla, and bivouaced. The head of the enemy's columns showed themselves in the plain before Ciudad Rodrigo. *Sept.* 24. The plain of Ciudad Rodrigo appeared filled with troops of the enemy, and a string of mules, etc., for many miles in extent entering the place. The enemy occupied Atalaga close to our front with two battalions of infantry and a regt. of cavalry.

NOTE.—The above operations are thus explained by Napier :— Ciudad Rodrigo wanted food, and Marmont arranged a combined operation for its succour, with the result that, on the 21st Sept. he had assembled 60,000 men, 6,000 being cavalry. On the 23rd, the French encamped to the north-east of the fortress, and a strong detachment, entering the plain, communicated with the garrison, examined the position of the Light Division, and returned. Next day, the whole of the French cavalry, and 4 divisions of infantry crossed the hills in two columns, and placing some troops in observation on the Vadillo introduced the convoy. Next day, (25th) the French advanced against the allies, and there ensued the combat of El Boden.

Reverting to the Diary :—*Sept.* 25. Soon after daylight a cannonade commenced upon our left towards Pastores, and continued till noon, when it became much warmer. Observed several movements of troops between El Boden and Pastores, on the other side of the Agueda. The firing appearing to advance towards the heights in front of Guinaldo, it was decided that our Division should withdraw from our position which appears hazardous. At 3 p.m., soon after orders had been given for that purpose, directions arrived from General Murray to the same effect. The rear of the division broke up at sunset, marched the greater part of the night, and bivouaced near this village (Cespedosa) being too much fatigued to reach Robleda as intended.

Sept. 26. Marched at daylight to Robleda ;—the ford of Canos, understood to be in the enemy's possession ; the Light Division crossed the Agueda at the ford of Penaparda, and moved into its post before Guinaldo by midday ; the enemy about a mile from our advanced posts in three large bodies, said to consist of 60,000 infantry and 5,000 cavalry; 22 battalions of the Imperial Guard were conspicuous amongst the crowd.

NOTE.—And yet, Napier states that—" the Light Division should have marched by Robledo to Guinaldo; Craufurd received the order at 3 o'clock, heard the cannonade, and might have reached Guinaldo before midnight; but fearing a night march he only moved to Cespedosa." And that, next day, the Light Division, " compelled to make a circuit, did not arrive till after 3 o'clock in the evening."

Sept. 27. So soon as it became dark last night, the army began to retreat, leaving the Light Division in Guinaldo until midnight, when we also retired; but the road was so crowded with baggage, etc., that it was daylight before we passed through Cossilas de Flores; continued our march to Furcalhas where we halted, our Division being ordered to take post there; but not finding any tenable ground, we moved into the position behind Aldea da Ponte, having the 4th Division upon our left, who were pushed by the enemy at dusk, which obliged us to stand to our arms several times, though we were not attacked.

Sept. 28. At 2 o'clock this morning retired from our position near the Convent of Sacapata through Alfayates, and bivouaced in the Chesnut wood close behind the village of Soita; drizzling rain all day. The French retired from Aldea da Ponte towards Ciudad Rodrigo, not choosing to attack us in this position.

NOTE.—Napier, commenting on the perilous situation of the Light Division during the night and morning of Sept. 25, and 26th, on the march to Guinaldo, states that, when Marmont heard of the escape of the Division, he—in allusion to Napoleon's fortune, prophetically exclaimed,—" And Wellington's star also is bright ! "

The French having retired, the Light Division, reinforced by some cavalry, resumed the nominal blockade of Ciudad Rodrigo in concert with Julian Sanchez, and the rest of the army was cantoned on both sides of the Coa, head-quarters being fixed at Frenada.

October 2. The Light Division moved into the Cantonment assigned to it, viz., Cossilos de Flores, Puebla da Azava, Castillego, and Fuente Guinaldo where Genl. Craufurd established his Head Qrs. I got the quarter formerly occupied by Col. Fletcher in the Marketplace. Head Qrs. said to be at Frenada over the Coa. *Oct.* 6. Riding over the scene of the action near El Boden with Genl. Craufurd, we started 2 hares, killed one and brought it home with us. *Oct.* 8. Coursed with the Genl. near El Boden, killed a young wolf or fox, and a hare. *Oct.* 14. The Governor of Ciudad Rodrigo taken and carried off by the Guerillas. *Oct.* 30. The Tragedy of Zanga performed by the officers of our Division in the Theatre, made in the Chapel near the town.

FUENTE GUINALDO, *Oct.* 9, 1811.

MY DEAR FATHER,

   . . . The *Gazette* will, long before you receive this, have made you acquainted with their (the enemy's) success in relieving Ciudad Rodrigo, and obliging us to retire from a position near this town, on the night of the 26th Ult., to another on the banks of the Coa, where it would seem we were to have awaited the enemy's attack, but where however they (having effected their object) did not choose to attack us. On the 25th they made a strong reconnaissance with their cavalry near El Boden, and were gallantly received by part of Genl. Picton's Div. and our Dragoons and Hussars, in consequence of whose rapid retreat our Division, 4 or 5 leagues in front and on the enemy's side of the Agueda, were for a short time completely cut off from the rest of the Army. Marching that night nevertheless enabled us to rejoin the Army in front of this town on the 26th; and on the night of the 26th, or rather, early on the 27th we formed the rear guard of the Army upon its retreat. In the evening they (enemy) came up to us, and attacking with great superiority of force, carried the hill upon which the Fusiliers (the 7th and 23rd) were posted; though, if I am not mistaken, they paid its full price before they occupied it. The next morning we took up a position near Saita, but there, as I said before, they did not care to follow. Accordingly in a day or two we advanced again, and have reoccupied this and the neighbouring places; Head Qrs. are at Frenedas, not far from Almeida.

I am rather surprised that Capt. Ellicombe has not yet reached Lisbon; everything appears so quiet, at least for several months, that I care not how soon he relieves me. As soon as we hear of his arrival I shall set out for Lisbon; but you cannot expect me in England in less than a month, or five weeks afterwards . . . yet it cannot be very long if we live, before I have the pleasure of seeing you, and of presenting to you *verba voce*, what I can only now do in writing; with assurances of my most dutiful love . . .

Your very loving son,
RICE JONES.

FUENTE GUINALDO, *October* 23, 1811.

MY DEAR FATHER,

My only inducement to write to you at this time, is to let you know that I am still waiting the arrival of Capt. Ellicombe at Lisbon, which surely cannot be delayed much longer. We continue precisely in the same state as when I wrote last. I am in as good, if not better health (Thank God) than I ever have been in this country; and was it not for the unpleasant state of suspense, that must of course continue until I set out for England, should be more comfortable also; for nothing can exceed the civility and attention of General Craufurd. . . . I am totally in the dark as to what is likely to be my future destination. There can be little doubt of my returning in a Packet, and consequently landing at

Falmouth. I calculated in a former letter that it would take about a month for me to reach England from the time of my quitting the army here.

You have, I daresay, already heard of General Reynaud, the French Governor of Ciudad Rodrigo, and a quantity of their cattle, being taken by Don Julian Sanchez's Spanish Guerillas; it has afforded us a good deal of amusement.

Nov. 3rd and 4th. Spent both days with Genl. Craufurd forming schemes to cut off the cattle the enemy send to graze daily; for which purpose we approached the place, often very near, upon all its sides. *Nov. 11.* General Craufurd still wishing to cut off the cattle from Ciudad Rodrigo, took me with him again to the hill near Pastores. Found their place of pasturage changed to the opposite bank of the Agueda. *Nov. 12.* Accompanied the Genl. in a minute reconnaissance of the ground from the road from La Caridade to that from Salamanca to Rodrigo, with a view to the execution of his scheme for intercepting the cattle when sent out to graze, returning to Fuente Guinaldo in the night.

Nov. 21. Col. Fletcher, Capt. J. T. Jones, Burgoyne and Mulcaster came to see Henry the 4th performed at our Theatre. They dined with me, and slept in my quarters.

NOTE.—And here, a short extract from Gleig's *Life of the Duke of Wellington*, may fitly find a place:—"Of toil and suffering, and danger too, the troops had from time to time enough; but every season of repose, and especially the winter, brought great enjoyment in its train, into which no one entered more heartily than the Duke of Wellington himself. . . . If Lord Wellington favoured one of the Divisions of the army more than the rest, it was the Light Division . . . the regiments composing it were models of all that good infantry ought to be; the men well drilled, the officers punctiliously attentive to the minutest details of duty, yet full withal of life and spirits. Among other accomplishments several of these young men possessed a decided talent for acting, and this winter they brought it into play."

Dec. 13. Accompanied Col. Fletcher to Almeida, which is repairing under Capt. MacCulloch's superintendence.

FUENTE GUINALDO, Nov. 20, 1811.

MY DEAR FATHER,

I have delayed writing until the last moment in hopes of hearing of Capt. Ellicombe's arrival at Lisbon. A Mail, with letters to the 16th Oct. arrived here yesterday; another day would have completed 8 full weeks without our getting either a letter or paper from England. The winds which caused this unparalleled blank in our communications has doubtless prevented the sailing of the vessel in which my expected relief is embarked; but if the fine, North-Easterly gale which has prevailed the last week or ten days will last a day or two longer, I think I shall hear of his arrival, in another week at the most; and may then, if I get a favourable passage, have the pleasure of eating my Christmas Dinner with my dear Father. We have not a word of news; things have as quiet an appearance as ever. My health, thank God, continues excellent. I wish much I could hear how you all are; but I fear you have, in the expectation of my more speedy return, given up writing to me altogether.

FUENTE GUINALDO, Dec. 4, 1811.

MY DEAR FATHER,

I was yesterday favoured with your letter of the 9th Ult. from Bristol. . . . The delay attending Capt. Ellicombe's reaching Lisbon is extraordinary; I believe he was ordered in the middle of August last— nearly 4 months ago, and the voyage does not commonly exceed a fortnight, but as yet we have not heard a syllable of him. I see by the Papers (which we have received to the 12th Oct. only) that several outward-bound convoys were at that time in Cowes Roads awaiting a favourable wind . . . and I conclude are at this moment at anchor in the Tagus. . . . Yet I must give up the idea I entertained when I last wrote, of being in England on Christmas Day—at least, reckoned by the New Style—by the old one, it is still possible. . . . We advanced, a few days ago, across the Agueda, to intercept a Convoy which was said to be on the point of entering Ciudad Rodrigo; but it did not appear at all, and we accordingly returned to our Cantonments here.

NOTE.—For some time past, Wellington's preparations for the Siege of Ciudad Rodrigo had been carried on unknown to the French; and Almeida was now being repaired to afford security for the siege stores and battering-train, which had been introduced, under pretence of being an armament for the new works. At the same time, a trestle-bridge to throw over the Agueda had been prepared secretly in the arsenal of Almeida. "Thus the preparations for the attack"—says Napier, "advanced while the English general seemed to be only intent upon defending his own positions." And he declares that not even the engineers employed in the preparations knew more than that a siege or the simulation of a siege was in contemplation; but when it was to be attempted, or that it would be attempted at all, none knew;—even the quarter-master general, Murray, was suffered to go home on leave with the full persuasion that no operation would take place before spring."

Reverting to the Diary :—

Fuente Guinaldo, Dec. 18. Received orders to prepare Fascines, etc., at the several quarters occupied by the Light Division. *Dec.* 20. Lord Wellington inspected the Division. *Martiago, Dec.* 23. Came

115

here, after setting the parties of the 43rd to work at fascine-making. *Dec.* 24. Gave directions to the 52nd, at Martiago and the neighbour-hood, to make fascines and gabions, and returned at night to Fuente Guinaldo. *Dec.* 25 (Xmas day). General Craufurd, Wood, and myself met General Stewart to course near Fuente de Onora, and dined with him. *Martiago, Dec.* 29. Inspected the parties of General Vandeleur's Brigade employed making fascines at Martiago, and slept there.

1812. *January 2.* Heavy snow this morning caused much inconvenience, and the subsequent postponement of the movements ordered for investing Ciudad Rodrigo. Went to Las Agallas to expedite the transport and collection of the fascines and gabions made by the Light Division.

Las Agallas, Jan., 1812.

My dear Father,

After such an extraordinary delay of my return to England, I fear the prospect is still rather distant; for although Capt. Ellicombe must undoubtedly have joined the Army before now, I have not as yet heard of his arrival; and the siege of Ciudad Rodrigo which it seems certain we shall now undertake, has, I doubt not, induced Lord Wellington to postpone my leaving the army until its termination, which will account for my not having heard from Col. Fletcher on the subject lately.

The armies of Marmont and D'Orsenne are said to be much separated and very distant; yet I fear they will advance and unite long before the completion of our labours, and oblige us to raise the siege—perhaps to recross the Coa. Our experience last summer at Badajoz has made me much less sanguine than I should otherwise feel at the prospect of a siege; but as we are now to be engaged in it, it is certainly much better that I should remain and see it out, than leave my brother officers in the midst of it. Let what will be the result, I have the satisfaction of knowing that my long procrastinated stay in this country, so far from being my own wish, has been quite contrary to my inclination; and I therefore most steadfastly rely upon the Providence which has hitherto attended my steps ordaining it all for the best.

We have for the last ten days been making Fascines and Gabions for the siege, and have this morning begun to move them to our Park before the place. It is some days since I have seen or heard from any of our officers, and I am therefore not aware when we break ground—I have heard to-morrow night, or the night after. I am afraid we shall experience very bad weather; we had a good deal of snow yesterday; but it is now fine again. . . . Adieu—and God bless you.

Your very loving son,
Rice Jones.

Note.—Once more, we must turn to the Historian for explanations:—" The favourable moment for action so long watched for by

Wellington came at last.   .   .   .   The Imperial Guards, 17,000 strong, being required by Napoleon for the Russian campaign, marched in December to France.   All the Polish battalions, and several thousand choice men destined to fill the ranks of the old guard were drafted ; so that not less than 40,000 of the best soldiers were withdrawn, and the maimed and worn-out men being sent to France at the same time, the force in the Peninsula was diminished by 60,000 men.   .   .   . Marmont also, deceived by the seeming careless winter attitude of the allies left Rodrigo unprotected and Wellington instantly jumped with both feet on the devoted fortress."

Jan. 8.   About noon, Ciudad Rodrigo was invested by the Light Division ; during the afternoon 269 cars arrived with tools, etc., from Gallegos, having crossed the Agueda by a bridge on trestles made by the Staff Corps.   A Park formed near the road, about 1,800 yds. from the place.   Soon after 8 o'clock in the evening Lieut. Thomson led a party commanded by Col. Colborne, to storm the new Redoubts, which was soon carried, and a party of 700 men set to work immediately—300 to form a lodgement in the Redoubt, and 400 to open a communication to it.   The enemy fired upon the redoubt all night.

NOTE.—Discussing Lord Wellington's extraordinary resourcefulness in emergencies, Mr. Larpent, the Judge Advocate-General of the army under his Lordship's command, writes in his Journal of the war :— " I heard an anecdote about the siege of Rodrigo which shows the man.   On a sudden the army was in front of it.   A new work had to be taken on the instant ; scaling ladders were necessary ; the Engineers had none,—being quite ignorant of the plans ; an inconvenience which has often arisen in different departments, from Lord W.'s great secrecy — though the general result, assisted by his genius has been so good.   Lord W. on being informed of this—" Well," said he, " You have brought up your ammunition and stores, never mind the waggons ; cut them all up directly, they will make excellent ladders— there, you see, each side-piece is already cut."   This was done, and the work scaled forthwith.

Major Dickson, (better known as Sir A. Dickson) an officer after Lord Wellington's own heart, wrote in his Diary, at the first siege of Badajoz, where he was entrusted by his Chief with the control of the artillery arrangements,—" I have transacted business with many generals, but never such a one as Lord Wellington, both for general knowledge, and attention to reason and suggestion."

Jan. 9.   400 men were employed all day to complete the work opened last night.   At night, the working parties consisted of 1,200, and the covering party of 500 ; the parallel was opened to its whole length, about 600 yds. ; and three batteries for 11 guns each were also begun.   Ross was killed early in the morning, near Battery

No. 1, reckoning from the left, by a shot from the Convent of San
Francisco.   (Brother of Ross of the Horse Artillery).

NOTE.—Details of this remarkable siege being fully given in Sir J. T.
Jones' work, we will pass on to the assault, in which exploit Rice
Jones took a prominent part :—

Jan. 19.   The breaches appearing practicable, a storm is determined upon.   A few minutes before 7 this evening the troops moved
to the assault.   Joined the Light Division, and by order of Genl.
Craufurd accompanied the advance under Major Napier.   After carrying the breach, a French officer conducted me to the Governor's house,
General Barrié, who was soon after brought in himself.   Having
taken possession of his Papers, etc., I left my orderly, Private Roger
O'Niel, to take care of them and the inhabitants of the house, and
returned to the Engineer Depòt.

NOTE.—We are fortunately enabled to supplement the Diarist's
all-too-brief account of the storming of Ciudad Rodrigo, by a somewhat
more detailed narrative of that dashing exploit contained in a letter
to his Father, written on the following day :—

CAMP BEFORE CIUDAD RODRIGO,

20th Jan., 1812.

MY DEAR FATHER,

I have barely sufficient time to acquaint you with the happy termination of our labours at the siege of Ciudad Rodrigo, by our carrying it
by assault yesterday evening.   The day after I wrote to you last from
Las Agallas we invested the place, took the new Redoubt of San Francisco and opened our First Parallel on the following days, we were so
highly favored by weather, and other circumstances, as to get possession
of the Suburbs and Convents, erect our Batteries and effect a practicable
breach yesterday evening.   In doing this we have met with considerable
loss ; amongst others my good friend George Ross was killed with
a splinter of a shell on his head ; soon after our commencement ;—no
man ever fell more universally regretted.   In storming the town last
night I fear our loss was great ;—and I am sorry to say my friend and
General (R. Craufurd) was dangerously wounded, yet I am happy to say
we are not without hope of his recovery.   I had the good fortune to lead
the 52nd and 43rd Regts. to a small breach, to the left of the large one
which General Picton entered, with little loss except Major Napier whom
I accompanied and who lost his arm.   We were together in the second
or third file, and were at first repulsed and driven headlong down the
breach ;—but shortly after tried again and gained it.   Thanks to the providence of that God upon whom I have always relied, I escaped this
rough treatment with a slight scratch of a bayonet on my thigh, and a
contusion on my breast, when I was pushed down the Breach :—which I
however feel not the slightest inconvenience from at present.   I shall be
very busy the next 3 or 4 days dismantling our batteries, and repairing

the breach :—after which I expect to set out on my return to England :—
when I hope for the pleasure of finding you all in good health.

From your very loving son,

RICE JONES.

The death of his friend is thus referred to by Southey, in his
History of the War :—" Capt. Ross of the Engineers was brother of
that excellent officer who afterwards fell at Baltimore, and was himself a man of great professional promise, uniting with military talents,
a suavity of manners, and a gentleness of disposition.   His friend and
comrade, Lt. Skelton, was killed at the same time and buried with
him in the same grave, in a little retired valley not far from the spot
where they fell.   Capt. Jones (the Historian of the war) placed a
small pedestal with an inscription to mark the grave, and with
prudent as well as Christian feeling, surmounted it with a cross.
That humble monument has, because of its Christian symbol, been
respected ; Spaniards have been seen kneeling there, and none pass it
without uncovering their heads."

Jan. 20.   The 5th Division under Genl. Leith occupied Ciudad
Rodrigo, and proceeded with all speed to fill up our works and
trenches ; after which, Lord Wellington gave Col. Fletcher permission to send me to England, agreeably to orders.   General Craufurd
buried with all possible honour at the foot of the breach.

NOTE.—The extreme severity of the conditions under which this
siege was conducted, will be understood when it is stated that—" the
period of the year was the commencement of January, when there is
more dark than daylight,"—I quote from the remarks of Sir J. T.
Jones, Royal Engineers, who was present as Brigade Major. "Secondly,
the weather was bitterly cold at night, and the ground frozen.   Thirdly,
the men employed to raise the batteries were on the march, or on
duty, for thirty hours consecutively ; and the troops, having to march
every morning from their different cantonments, six or eight miles
distant from the trenches, were fatigued before they began to work."
And what made it all the more trying was that many of the troops
had to cross the river nearly up to their shoulders, and remain in this
wet state until they returned to their quarters.   It is not surprising,
therefore, that " as whilst they remained on duty they could not take
any rest from the extreme cold, they became worn out and incapable
of any exertion long before the expiration of their tour of 24 hours'
work, which materially impeded the progress of the work."   In spite
of all these drawbacks, Sir J. T. Jones tells us that every man felt
confident of success, and acted accordingly.   Patient and indefatigable
at work, impetuous and daring in the assault, they shone throughout
this siege in their proper light, and gave strong proofs of possessing
superior qualities for such undertakings."

CIUDAD RODRIGO, *Jan.* 28, 1812.

MY DEAR FATHER,

At length everything is settled so as to allow of my returning to England, and to-morrow morning I intend setting out for Lisbon, where I expect to arrive about the 8th Feby. I shall not be able to leave Lisbon in less than a week, which will make it the 16th before I can probably embark, and with the blessing of God and a fair wind, I may have the pleasure of landing in England a fortnight afterwards; I continue, thank God, in excellent health and spirits, and if we are favoured with more of the beautifully fine weather we have had of late, the march to Lisbon will be by no means disagreeable. But I have such an aversion to the sea that I cannot say I look with so much satisfaction at the prospect of the voyage—short, even as it is.

Since I wrote last week, we have been busily employed, levelling the works we had raised against the place; re-forming and enlarging the Redoubts we stormed the first night; and repairing the two breaches in the main wall, all of which is now completed, or very nearly, at least, so as to place this city in a state of security from assault.

The French army which Marmont had assembled at Salamanca, for the relief of this place, after pushing some small corps about 6 or 7 leagues from hence, have, it is said, retired again behind the Tormes.

Poor General Craufurd, after severe suffering from his wounds, expired on the 24th Inst. In him I have lost a warm and valuable friend, and the Army one of its bravest, and most scientific officers. Few had the opportunity of forming a just estimate of his real worth, except those who lived at his hospitable table, and saw him in his quiet and domestic moments. . . .

Your very affectionate son,

RICE JONES.

Jan. 30. Bade farewell to the army I have served with so long, and proceeded on my way to Lisbon.

Feb. 16. Embarked in the *Lady Arabella*, Packet, Capt. Porteous; got under weigh about 7 o'clock next morning; blowing tempestuously which soon carried us out of sight of the coast. Came to anchor in Falmouth at 11 o'clock at night, on the 24th. Set off at 2 a.m., next morning in the Mail from Falmouth; breakfasted at Truro, dined at Launcestown, and slept at Exeter. Disagreeable weather;—wind and sleet; very cold on the Downs. There being no place to be had inside the Mail at Exeter, I rode on the outside as far as Salisbury, where I took the place of another passenger and travelled all night. *Feb.* 27. Arrived in London greatly fatigued and exhausted by my journey. *March* 25. Commenced to do duty at Woolwich.

NOTE.—The rest of the Diary being chiefly concerned with matters of family interest, need not detain us.

A TARDY RECOGNITION.

On the 17th July, 1847, an official communication, addressed to "Colonel R. Jones, The Commanding Royal Engineer, Gibraltar," to the following effect, was received :—

"Colonel Rice Jones is requested to forward to this Office the statement herein required, addressed to the Secretary of the Board of General officers, specifying the Battles or Actions for which he has received a medal."

GENERAL ORDER.   No. 582.

Horse Guards,
1st *June*, 1847.

28th *June*, 1847.

Her Majesty having been graciously pleased to command that a Medal should be struck to record the Services of Her Fleets and Armies during the Wars commencing in 1793, and ending in 1814, and that one should be conferred upon every Officer, Non-Commissioned Officer, and Soldier of the Army, who was present in any Battle or Siege, to commorate which Medals had been struck by command of Her Majesty's Royal Predecessors, and had been distributed to the General, or Superior, Officers of the several Armies and Corps of Troops engaged, in conformity with the Regulations of the Service at that time in force ;— General and other Officers, Non-Commissioned Officers, and Soldiers, who consider that they have claims to receive this Mark of their Sovereign's gracious recollection of their Services, and of Her desire to record the same, are each to apply to the Secretary of the Board of General Officers, Whitehall, London, and to send in writing to the same Officer, a statement of his claim, for what action at what period of time, and the Names of the persons, or the title of the Documents by which the claim can be proved.

(Here follow instruction with reference to the submission of claims).

.   .   .   .   .   .

The occasions, for which Medals have been granted by the Sovereign, are specified in the annexed page for general information and guidance, as at page 73 of the *Annual Army List*.

By Command of Field Marshal,
The Duke of Wellington,
Commander-in-chief.

John Macdonald,
Adjutant-General.

Honorary Distinctions have been granted to officers in Commemoration of their Services in the following Battles or Actions :—

Maida	4 July, 1806	Badajoz... ... { 17 March / 6 April } 1812
Roleia	17 August, 1808	
Vimiera... ...	21 August, 1808	Salamanca ... 22 July, 1812
Sahagun, Benevente { Dec , 1808 / Jan., 1809 }		Fort Detroit, America August, 1812
		Vittoria... ... 21 June, 1813
Corunna ...	16 Jany., 1809	Pyrenees ... { 28 July / to 2 Aug. } 1813
Martinique	...Feby., 1809	
Talavera ...	27, 28 July, 1809	St. Sebastian ... Aug., Sept., 1813
Guadaloupe ...	Jany., Feb., 1810	Chateau Guay, America 26 Oct., 1813
Busaco	27 Sept., 1810	Nivelle ... ... 10 Nov., 1813
Barrosa... ...	5 March, 1811	Chrystler's Farm, America
Fuentes d'Onor...	5 May, 1811	11 Nov., 1813
Albuhera ...	16 May, 1811	Nive ... ...9 to 13 Dec., 1813
Java ...	Aug. and Sept., 1811	Orthes ... ... 27 Feb., 1814
Ciudad Rodrigo	January, 1812	Toulouse ... 10 April, 1814

The following reply was forwarded, in response to the above GENERAL ORDER :—

"Statement of the several Battles and Sieges enumerated in the Genl. Order, dated, H. Gds., 1 June, 1847, No. 582, at which Colonel Rice Jones was present, and for which a medal is claimed :—

Talavera ... ...27 and 28 July, 1809
Busaco ... ... 27 Sept., 1810
Albuhera ... ...16 May, 1811
Ciudad Rodrigo ... January, 1812

Under the late Lt.-Col. Fletcher, Comdg. R. Engs. with the army in the Peninsula.

R.J.

Other Publications from pagesofpages.com on Wellington

See:
https://www.pagesofpages.com/publ/wellington/wellington.html

Most volumes available in paper, 6 by 9 inches, at $24.95 each, and as Kindle e-books ($4.95 to $7.95).

The Dispatches, Gurwood's New edition of 1837-1839.

India Volumes,
Volume One. Apr 5, 1799 - Jun 12, 1803. 979-8741570364
Volume Two. Jun 12, 1803 - Jan 24, 1804. 979-8745952722
Volume Three. Jan 24, 1804 - Apr 2, 1805. 979-8749840094

The Peninsula
Volume Four. Aug 1808 – Sep 13, 1809. 979-8419409545
Volume Five. August 1809 – March 1810. 979-8424514678
Volume Six. April 1810 – Nov 1810. 979-8437029992

Waterloo, The Occupation of Paris
Volume Twelve. May 1, 1814 - Nov 30, 1815. 979-8408046348

The Supplementary Despatches

India Volumes
Volume One. Apr 11, 1797 - Jun 6, 1800. 979-8738806483
Volume Two. Jun 6, 1800 - Dec 11, 1801. 979-8742145523
Volume Three. Dec 14, 1801 - Feb 14, 1803. 979-8743336500
Volume Four. Feb 15, 1803 -1805. *Only available as a Kindle e-book.*

Waterloo, The Occupation of Paris
Volume Ten. Mar to July, 1815. ISBN 979-8414609483.

Index
Volume 15. Index. *Available as a Kindle e-book only.*

www.ingramcontent.com/pod-product-compliance
Lightning Source LLC
Chambersburg PA
CBHW051843130726
47987CB00002B/661